bedrooms

bedrooms

CREATING AND DECORATING THE ROOM OF YOUR DREAMS

MARY GILLIATT

jacqui small

First published in 2007 by Jacqui Small LLP,
an imprint of Aurum Press, 7 Greenland Street, London NW1 0ND

Text copyright © Mary Gilliatt 2007
Photography, design and layout copyright © Jacqui Small 2007

ISBN-10: 1 903221 92 7
ISBN-13: 978 1 903221 92 1

A catalogue record for this book is available from the British Library.

2010 2009 2008
10 9 8 7 6 5 4 3 2 1

Printed in China

PUBLISHER Jacqui Small
EDITORIAL MANAGERS Kate John, Judith Hannam
DESIGNER Ashley Western
EDITOR Hilary Mandleberg
PRODUCTION Peter Colley
PICTURE RESEARCH Nadine Bazar

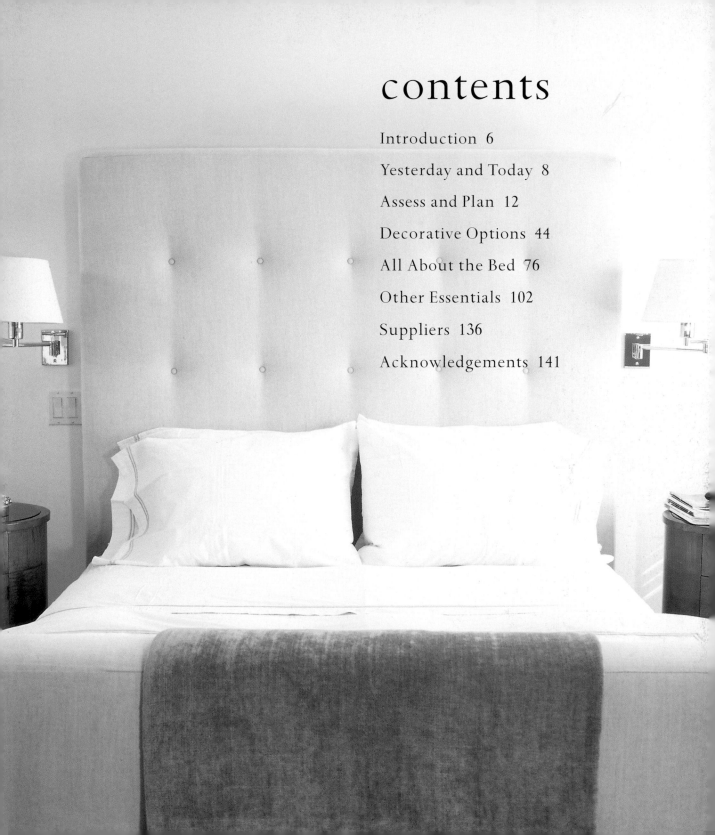

contents

'Oh bed! Oh Bed! Delicious Bed! That Heaven upon earth to the weary head!' This seductive sentiment expressed by the nineteenth-century English poet, Thomas Hood, is both timeless and universal, although it turns out that most people of Hood's time, whatever their status, however well-furnished their bedrooms and however delicious their feather beds, were plagued by decidedly un-delicious fleas and bedbugs. Even as late as the end of Queen Victoria's reign in 1901, one firm was advertising itself as 'Bug Destroyers to Her Majesty'. Happily, the majority of beds are now wholly bug-free. Thanks to the universality of baths and showers, not to mention washing machines and tumble dryers, bedroom cleanliness has improved enormously. And most people – apart from the puritanical who are wary of anything sybaritic and are uncomfortable with comfort – treasure their bedrooms as much as their sleep.

Nevertheless, as late as the 1960s, the President of the National Bedding Federation announced that the British were very parsimonious about their beds: 'We place luxurious sleeping equipment at everybody's disposal,' he complained, 'but many people are still sleeping, or trying to sleep, on beds and mattresses in the last stages of senile decay.' Interestingly, the president's point still prevails some half a century later, and not just among the British. People all over the world change their cars, even their homes, much more often than their mattresses. But since the 1960s, the role of the bedroom has changed. It is now a multi-functional room. What we now need, therefore, is a wide choice of design options not just for beguiling bedrooms and guest rooms, but for bedrooms-cum-studies-cum-home offices, bedrooms-cum-exercise rooms, bedrooms-cum-sitting rooms and children's bedrooms-cum-playrooms.

OPPOSITE A fur throw and a mass of cushions make this bed look completely 'delicious'. The muted colour scheme and the comfortable upholstery add to the extremely enticing effect. The Chinese panels hanging above each bedside table balance the bulk of the bed and help create a modern Oriental mood.

YESTERDAY AND TODAY

Multi-functional bedrooms, are of course, not new although they now serve somewhat different functions from the bedroom-cum-receiving room-cum-card room-cum-supper room and -cum-more intimate sitting room that grandee families once possessed. Then the bed was generally one of the most important and costly pieces of furniture in the house, and, with its carved frame, canopy and hangings, was practically a room within a room. Quite frequently, at least until the end of the eighteenth century, monarchs and senior nobles would receive subjects or morning callers reclining on top of their mattresses – usually fully dressed. However, when the bed was not being used for receptions, the bed curtains were kept closed since the sight of the actual bedclothes was considered unseemly.

Today's bedrooms, can, if they are spacious enough, also take on other roles. Children's rooms are more often than not used for play, homework

THIS PAGE A contemporary bedroom with stark white marble walls and floor is pared down to a few details – an understated bed, a pair of wall lights, a black chest and minimal accessories.

OPPOSITE A handsome carved four-poster bed in a stone-walled room is complemented by furniture of the seventeenth century and a replica nineteenth-century stove.

and entertaining friends as well as for sleep, while guest rooms are sometimes used as studies, exercise rooms, and even as occasional dining rooms. But in the twenty-first century, master bedrooms are invariably private to their occupants and immediate family, and are only also general reception rooms if they form an integral part of a studio or one-room apartment.

WHAT 24-HOUR BEDROOMS NEED

With so many bedrooms now, therefore, on 24-hour duty, they must provide 24-hour comfort. This does not only mean comfortable beds and bedding, or comfortable chairs, sofas and flooring, but nowadays also means having state-of-the-art wiring to accommodate versatile lighting, heating and ventilation, as well as telephone lines, alarm systems, entertainment systems, computing and printing equipment, and internet access. You may also also need efficient sound insulation. In addition, comfort entails having generous, well-organized storage to suit all the users of the bedroom and all the uses to which the bedroom is put.

Only when those background necessities to comfortable living are in place should you finally concentrate on the decoration. This, as well as being good-looking, should be appropriate in terms of budget

OPPOSITE BELOW LEFT
A comfortable modern bed stands on a base that incorporates discreet bedside tables. Wall lights above are perfect for reading in bed.

OPPOSITE BELOW RIGHT
In a gentle period-style bedroom, the delicate wrought-iron headboard is complemented by the understated pictures on the wall above. Bleached-out fabrics do not jar.

BELOW LEFT Lightweight fabric panels are simply attached to beams above the pair of windows. The comfortably cushioned bed, set between the windows, contrasts with the high ceiling with its rough beams.

BELOW RIGHT A tassel-looped classical print forms the backdrop to an ornate cast-iron daybed in a room with a period feel.

and the style and location (town or country) of your home. If you attend to the decoration too soon, you may well find that it has to be re-done at a later date to accommodate forgotten necessities.

As well as describing how to plan for all these background elements and giving seductive examples for decorating according to a variety of tastes and budgets, this book also discusses how to make the best use of the space you have, and how to choose beds, mattresses, bedding, wall and floor finishes, window treatments and lighting, storage and accessories. And finally, it suggests where to go for what by offering contact details for suppliers of your bedroom requisites.

Assess and Plan

THIS PAGE Sliding sandblasted glass doors are both space-saving and rather chic. They also maximize the natural light, allowing it to pass through from the large bedroom window into the next room.

As an interior designer, I always find it sensible to start with the client's ideal and work backwards in the light of the size and proportion of the rooms, the needs of the occupants, the location of the home, the climate and last, but far from least, a realistic budget based on thorough research. In the case of a bedroom, whether this is a master bedroom, a guest room or a child's room, I weigh up the pros and cons of the available rooms then I look around and see if any room other than the current bedroom might provide a more satisfactory space to allow for, say, better storage, an en-suite bathroom, if there is not already one, or simply more space. Exactly the same thought processes apply if you are not employing an interior decorator. You need to be clear about you and your family's priorities and needs. You must ensure that the bedroom is located in the most appropriate room of your home. You must consider the needs of the bedroom in terms of lighting, wiring, sound insulation, warmth and ventilation, and you must think about your storage requirements. And all of this must be considered in the context of your budget. While such details may appear to be tedious when it is the actual decoration and furnishing that you are looking forward to, it is important to realise that you cannot start on those until you have a proper plan and you cannot plan properly until you have done the groundwork. It is as simple as that.

THIS PAGE A comfortable padded headboard has a practical cover that can be removed for ease of cleaning.

OPPOSITE ABOVE LEFT In designer Catherine Memmi's house, a shower area, storage, good lighting, and a comfortable bed are all provided in one single bedroom space.

OPPOSITE ABOVE RIGHT With its floor-to-ceiling bookshelves creating an alcove for the bed, this room is as much library as bedroom.

OPPOSITE BELOW LEFT Bunk beds fitted into an alcove provide cosy, space-saving sleeping quarters for two children.

OPPOSITE BELOW RIGHT Twin beds are placed beneath a long, low rectangular window which gives a headboard effect in a small, spare guest room. A pair of low-hanging pendant lights are both decorative and practical for bedtime reading.

WHAT DO YOU NEED?

Because of the limitations on space that exist today, especially in urban areas, many of us need a multi-purpose bedroom. Some of us want our bedroom to serve as a bathing area as well as a place to sleep. We do not all have space for a bedroom and an en-suite bathroom but, thanks to the many attractive, space-saving shower 'pods' that are now on the market, we might be able to squeeze a shower into the bedroom itself. Whichever bathing option your space allows, make sure that you can install adequate plumbing and drainage and, if needed, a soil pipe for a lavatory. If you want a really efficient shower, you will either require good headroom between the water tank and the shower, or you will have to install a pump.

Another possible use for the bedroom is as a home office or study. In this case, in addition to storage for clothes, you will need shelves for books, drawers for small items and somewhere to put files and papers. Your home-office requirements must also include a desk or a work surface that is roomy

enough not only to work at and have your paper and stationery requisites close at hand, but that has space for a computer, printer, phone and perhaps also a scanner and fax machine. You will also need a comfortable desk chair and you should bear in mind that, at the end of the day, you may want to be able to put everything away so that your bedroom can once more become a room for calm and sleep.

Remember, too, that furniture is not all you need to consider for the bedroom-cum-office. You must also make sure that you have plenty of power outlets as well as a telephone line for your internet and fax.

RELAXATION AND EXERCISE

Another popular option is a bedroom-cum-home entertainment room. This means ensuring that you have sufficient power sockets and space for the plasma screen, speakers, DVD collection and possibly also a CD collection, though many of us now have our music stored on an MP3 player or on our computer. If you plan to watch television from bed, make sure the screen is at the correct viewing height and distance.

You might, though, wish to combine your bedroom with a space for exercising. Most exercise equipment takes up a lot of room and can be very overpowering, so if possible, consider adding a screen or half-wall to hide it from view when not in use.

BEDROOMS FOR OTHER PEOPLE

Sometimes the bedroom you are planning is not for your own use at all. If it is a child's bedroom that you need, see pages 64–67, which offer some specific advice for such a room. If it is a guest room, turn to pages 68–69 to find some useful tips and pointers.

LEFT A contemporary moulded plywood screen would be perfect for hiding exercise equipment or an office zone from the sleeping area in a multi-purpose bedroom.

OPPOSITE A quite chic-looking filing cabinet used as a bedside table would be suitable for a bedroom-cum-home office. This would be a good solution where space is limited and the office function needs to be subservient to that of the restorative bedroom.

LOCATION, LOCATION

BELOW This stunning bedroom makes the most of its woodland outlook with an entire wall of sliding glass doors. Unpainted wooden window frames and a wooden floor help to underline the link with the outdoors.

Remote though the possibility may seem to people with smallish homes and similarly sized budgets some, at least, of your ideals might be easier to attain than at first imagined. Unless you are confident that you can achieve most of what you want with your current room arrangement, try to see if re-thinking that arrangement could make a difference. We are so used to accepting the status quo, the placement and role of rooms on a given floor of a house, that many of us would not even think of relocating the bedroom entirely or of knocking two rooms into one and then starting again to create one room that is large enough to accommodate good storage, an en-suite bathroom and any non-bedroom activities that we may require, or that, with the help of partitions, can become a bedroom suite.

OPPOSITE In order not to lose any of the view of the steep mountainside, the owner has taken part of the window frame down to floor level and has continued the window around the corner of the room. Curtains would completely spoil the effect, so this would not suit someone who hates morning light.

RELOCATING THE BEDROOM

If you live in a house, it might be that you could move the living room to the floor above and use the freed-up space downstairs for a large en-suite bedroom and bathroom, or even for a suite of rooms. Or, if you have a townhouse with a well-ventilated basement, and if you do not crave morning light, then that too, might be a good place to locate the bedroom suite. Often such a basement is occupied by the kitchen, but why not create a more light-filled kitchen elsewhere and re-allocate the space to a bedroom? Or, if you have a large attic, you might be able to create a bedroom, bathroom,

dressing room or walk-in storage and study space up there. In some instances, you might have a room with a high enough ceiling to create a mezzanine for the sleeping area with maybe a study/home office/ parents' sitting room or bathroom down below.

OPENING UP THE SPACE

Check out partition walls everywhere in your home. They are usually easier to remove than you might think and their removal could help you create a much more convenient space. There is also the possibility that some load-bearing walls can be successfully removed,

OPPOSITE FAR LEFT
Shades of grey might normally be unwelcoming in a bedroom, but this suite of rooms in an Italian villa benefits from good light and high ceilings.

OPPOSITE ABOVE A plastic concertina wall runs along a ceiling track and divides off the bed area in a generously windowed studio, made lighter still by its whiteness.

OPPOSITE BELOW A small space, just large enough to accommodate a bed, is curtained off from the rest of the room.

RIGHT Lofty floor-to-ceiling pivoting polycarbonate screens divide a vividly coloured sleeping area from the living area in a sleek, minimalist space.

as long as you insert the proper support instead, such as RSJs (rolled steel joists) disguised as columns.

If good light is lacking in your room, would it help to have a bigger window or an extra window, assuming, of course, that you do not contravene any planning regulations? Or might you find that simply changing the position of a door or changing the direction in which it opens results in more easily arrangeable space?

EXPAND THE SPACE YOU HAVE

Even if your master bedroom is not en-suite with a bathroom and you must keep it where it is, see if there is space to create a small but workable bathroom or shower room. If it is en-suite already, perhaps there is space for a dressing room or study. These might be achieved by using part of the bedroom itself, by using part of an adjoining bedroom or landing, or sometimes by converting a particularly large cupboard space.

LOCATION OF CHILDREN'S ROOMS

Still thinking out of the box, do your children occupy the best room or rooms for their needs, and how do you plan to accommodate children you hope to have in the future? Might your children, for example, be better

BELOW LEFT A room with plenty of ceiling height is perfect for locating a sleeping platform. Accessed by a simple ladder, you will need to be nimble to reach it, but there is no doubt that it is a space-saving solution.

BELOW RIGHT Proving that you do not really need more than an alcove to sleep in, this cosy corner of a multi-purpose space provides the bare necessities.

off having the current master bedroom as a bedroom-cum-playroom, while you relocate the master bedroom or bedroom suite to the former children's rooms? Or, if you have only one child's room and you are either expecting another child or want to give your child a play area, could that child's room be divided by a double-sided storage wall with a 'doorway' through?

WHERE TO MAKE A GUEST ROOM

You may have to use your imagination to find space for guest quarters. In some instances I have even seen an alcove or landing used. If you have no separate room to spare, consider making the living room or a study double up, by adding a comfortable sofa bed with a side table and a lamp. The place for clothes storage need be no more than an empty drawer and some discreet hooks on the back of the door.

ABOVE There is just space here, on a platform under the eaves, for a double bed and bedside table, positioned to look straight out of the window in a guest room in the Rockies. The more limited the space, the more comfortable the bed, bedding and pillows need to be so there is no sense of confinement or constriction. Here the naïve design of the quilt and the rough log that serves as a bedside table underline the log-cabin feel of the bedroom.

ABOVE RIGHT In a Mediterranean house, an alcove has a built-in day-bed that is perfect for lazy daytime relaxation as well as for occasional guests for night-time use. With its brightly striped cover and comfortable cushions, it provides a splash of colour in an all-white room.

RIGHT A small space under the eaves and in front of a dormer window in designer Catherine Memmi's house, still has just enough room for a comfortable double bed. The windowsill behind is a perfect substitute for a bedside table and sleek floor lamps provide the necessary lighting for bedtime reading.

ASSETS

If you are keeping your existing bedroom and do not want to embark on any major structural alterations, take some time to assess the room's pluses and minuses. Often, if you have used a room for a long time, you get immune to its advantages and disadvantages. You might be pleasantly surprised at the changes you could make without too much cost and upheaval.

First think about the lighting. Can the natural light be improved simply by removing heavy curtains and swapping them for a simpler window treatment? What is the state of the flooring? Is there a potentially beautiful floor lurking beneath a tired old carpet? Could you remove the carpet and give the floor a facelift, or would just an extra rug or two help? Are there any interesting architectural details? If not, consider adding a cornice or extra moulding to door frames and skirting boards to make them more impressive. Do the wardrobe interiors accommodate your requirements or would some new interior fitments make the difference you need?

ABOVE Here the owners have taken advantage of the lovely outdoor space by locating their bedroom so they can walk straight outside via the sliding glass door. The simple scheme does not detract from the view outside nor from the attractive old beamed ceiling. The contemporary chair and footstool add a nice touch.

RIGHT A working fireplace is an undoubted asset in any room but it adds an especially cosy touch to a bedroom. The decoration of the room, though it has a period feel to match the fireplace, has been kept deliberately pared-down and simple so the fireplace can take centre stage.

THIS PAGE The upper rooms in large period homes frequently suffer from low ceilings as this was often where the servants slept. Here, a ceiling has been removed to reveal the roof beams and give additional height. The unadorned four-poster bed allows a clear view of the room's attractive structure. Simple lightweight window blinds suit the room's spare style as well as allowing in maximum daylight.

BUDGET

Budgeting is always slightly chicken-and-egg. It first involves getting builders' estimates or at least having an idea of the cost of materials and of labour. The sort of work you might be contemplating could be structural, such as demolishing partition or even structural walls, building new partition walls, adding, enlarging or blocking up windows, and improving plumbing, wiring, lighting, insulation, heating and ventilation.

After that come wall and floor finishes, and fixtures such as baths, basins and showers if you are planning an en-suite bathroom. Then there is the bed, mattress and headboard, not to mention window treatments, which must include both the cost of the materials and the labour charges, storage furniture, whether off-the-peg or bespoke, other furniture, light fixtures and fittings, entertainment equipment, soft furnishings and accessories. Checking out these costs will involve you in a great deal of time and window shopping.

Once you have costed out what, ideally you would like to have, you should add on ten per cent as a contingency. No matter how well you plan, there are always unforeseen costs to be catered for. Now, depending on just

ABOVE Here minimalism is the epitome of quality, from the shiny, resin-coated floor, to the matching bed surround and shelf with its discreet speakers.

ABOVE LEFT An old white-painted iron bedstead with crisp white sheets and pillowcases in a simple, all-white room is stylish and won't break the bank.

OPPOSITE The main blow-the-budget items in this room are the mahogany sleigh bed and the chandelier. Two pairs of French doors opening onto balconies add a sense of spaciousness and luxury at no cost.

how big your budget is, you may be fortunate and be able to accommodate all these costs. You may also be able to afford to use an interior decorator, and buy the best possible materials and the fixtures and fittings that your heart desires.

SMALL-BUDGET OPTIONS

If, however, having reached this point, you find that you cannot afford exactly what you want, you have three options; either do as much of the work as possible yourself, have second and third choices in mind if your first prove too expensive, or stagger the work. This means deciding what is essential to be done now and what you can add later. Drawing up a staggered plan spread over a couple of years or more will enable you to work within a pre-determined annual budget.

However, if there is any essential structural work to do, you must not be tempted to do a cosmetic job now – unless it can be done really inexpensively. It is far better to save for that structural work and have it done as soon as you can afford it as otherwise any money you spend on decoration beforehand will be wasted.

Finally, if you are not fortunate enough to have much money to spend on your bedroom update, or if, perhaps, you are living in rented accommodation and do not want to spend money on a room that you do not own, do not despair. People with small budgets are usually forced to compromise, and compromise is often one of the best spurs to creativity. For instance, it is surprising how the perception of space can be changed simply by moving the furniture around. Similarly, using colour in an imaginative way can entirely change the way a room looks. Or, you might try drawing attention to, say, just the bed, by dressing it as lavishly as you can afford (see pages 94–101). With that as your bedroom's focal point, you may not notice the rest.

THIS PAGE This room is clearly influenced by the best hotel rooms. The deeply buttoned headboard, generous velvet curtains, comfortable upholstered chairs and sleek custom-made bedside tables are certainly at the pricier end of the market.

THE COMFORT ZONE

A comfortable bedroom requires to be well-illuminated, warm in winter and cool in summer. Nowadays, the bedroom is also often a place to watch television or listen to music, not to mention perhaps also serving as a home office.

Although good lighting is so important to both wellbeing and comfort, it is often the last thing people think of when they are planning a room. This is unfortunate as it is costly and disruptive to install extra wiring, switches and power sockets once the structural work and decoration have been finished.

In the main part of the bedroom, your lighting plan should include general or ambient light. You will also need task lighting to read by and light for putting on make-up or for shaving, if you perform these functions in the bedroom. Task lighting also includes lighting inside cupboards and wardrobes. It is irritating not to see where your clothes and shoes are.

Finally there is accent or decorative lighting. You may have a beautiful picture or vase that you want as a focal point, or you might like to create a dramatic effect with concealed lighting, perhaps behind a false ceiling, above a run of cupboards or below the bed.

Never underestimate the number of sockets and switches and the amount of wiring you will need. There is nothing worse — nor more dangerous — than having a bedroom with lots of trailing wires. These always indicate that the wiring has been badly planned.

Thus, as well as ceiling lights, you may want wall lamps, which might include lamps alongside a make-up mirror; table lamps for bedside tables, desks and dressing tables; floor lamps (which may be served by a power socket in the floor); and the always- invaluable lights inside cupboards. In addition, you may need wiring for the television, DVD player, music system and speakers; power sockets for an electric clock or clock-

OPPOSITE Good bedroom lighting sets the scene. Here ambient light is provided by cleverly positioned dimmable spotlights above the bed, while the lamps either side of the bed light the paintings above as well as casting light down for reading. The cantilevered bedside tables have integral lighting to illuminate the floor beneath them.

RIGHT Comfort today usually includes a television. In this gleaming white semi open-plan apartment in a Manhattan town house, a television has been incorporated in the wall dividing the bedroom from the dining area. If you are planning to have a television in the bedroom, ensure that all the wiring is in place before you decorate.

radio; for a computer and its associated paraphernalia; for a telephone, a burglar alarm and a baby alarm.

Also consider having two-way switches installed, to enable you to switch on bedside lamps both from the bedroom door and from the bed. Dimmer switches are another useful adjunct in the bedroom where you don't always want the lighting to be at full strength.

HEATING AND VENTILATION

It is at the planning stage that you need to consider heating and ventilation. Radiators provide the heating in most homes these days, so you need to decide how many you need, how large they must be to supply the heat you require, where to locate them and what type to use. These are complex decisions so it will pay you to seek some specialist advice.

Today's radiators come in all shapes and sizes. There are those that are slimline and relatively unobtrusive, those that hug the skirting board or are set in a channel along the edge of the wall, retro-style radiators that were once dumped in skips and are now *de rigueur* for their industrial-chic look, and super-modern designs that look like pieces of coiled wire. When it comes to looks, that will be largely down to personal taste, though some types are more efficient than others. Make sure you do your homework.

Another heating option to consider is underfloor heating. Though mostly installed at the building stage, some can be installed in isolation. The advantage of underfloor heating, of course, is that it is totally unobtrusive and does not take up valuable wall space.

When it comes to keeping a room cool in summer, the ultimate is air-conditioning but a ceiling fan with different speed settings is a more low-tech – and less costly – option. And if the worst comes to the worst, you can always open a window!

THIS PAGE In a room in a house in Australia that is almost devoid of colour, any details tend to stand out. The radiator has been chosen for its sleek, unobtrusive lines.

OPPOSITE LEFT A large window together with a ceiling fan above the bed keep this room feeling as cool and airy as it looks.

OPPOSITE RIGHT A slim-finned radiator beneath the window keeps this room in an Italian villa nicely warm in winter, while the three generous windows keep it just as nicely cool in summer.

STORAGE PLANNING

Bedroom storage needs good advance planning if it is to be successful. Your first step when planning should be to make a list of everything you have to find a home for. You will need the obvious hanging, drawer and shelf space for clothes and shoes, but you should not forget sporting equipment, luggage, books, CDs and DVDs, winter and summer bedlinen and whatever else your bedroom arrangements require. You must also consider what things you need to be able to access on a daily basis, what you require, say, once a week, and those items that you may only need once a year, such as seasonal bedding. Items that you use less frequently can obviously be stored in more out-of-the way places.

Next you must decide the best way to provide adequate storage space for your possessions without spoiling the proportions of the room. One of the

ABOVE LEFT This tiny en-suite bathroom has a space-saving lacquered vanity unit incorporating cupboards and drawers.

LEFT Extra storage is provided here by a well-coordinated selection of 1950s furniture – the night stand, chest of drawers and bookshelf at the foot of the bed.

OPPOSITE A whole wall of closet space with sliding doors provides good, space-saving storage in this neatly planned room. The reflective surface of the doors helps to make the narrow space feel bigger than it really is.

best solutions is built-in, made-to-measure storage. It is expensive and you cannot take it with you if you move, but it makes the best use of every bit of space. As well as installing floor-to-ceiling wall fitments, in which you could leave space for the bed and bedside tables or for a mirror and make-up area, consider using the space around, above and below windows and around and above doors. If you are seriously short of space, try having your bed built on a platform that is high enough to incorporate some deep drawers or buy an ottoman-style bed with storage beneath.

Another option, if your room is spacious enough, is to build a storage wall behind the bed. It acts as a tall headboard on one side, but go around it and you will find useful walk-in storage on the other.

Yet another option involves using part of an adjoining room or rooms or part of an adjoining landing for extra bedroom storage. Here, you might be able to gain a slither of space sufficient to make a walk-in dressing room. Fit it with rods for hanging clothes, and with shoe racks and banks of drawers for underwear, folded items of clothing and accessories.

Finally, since storage space is always at such a premium, you should scan every corner of your bedroom to make sure you are maximizing its potential. Do not ignore the back of the door. Hooks can take dressing gowns, outdoor coats and jackets. And even if you don't have built-in under-bed storage, you can always use some off-the-peg roll-out drawers or, at the very least, under-bed mesh or plastic bags.

THIS PAGE A well-planned bedroom with the bed situated opposite the door and positioned to make the most of the natural daylight. The bed is adorned with a patchwork quilt and a mass of cushions in warm, spicy colours, which make it look very inviting.

- A good scale for a bedroom plan is 1:50. which means that 2cm will represent 1m (¼in represents 1 foot).

- You will need a sharp pencil, a long retractable tape measure, a ruler, a rubber and graph paper.

- To include furniture, first make graph paper cut-outs to scale. Arrange them on the plan as you wish before drawing them in.

- It helps at the planning stage to include proposed new sockets and switches.

- Plans of each wall will help you calculate paint and wallpaper requirements.

Drawing Up a Room Plan

Whether you are planning a bedroom from scratch or simply redecorating and refurnishing a bedroom, mistakes of scale and furniture placement can be avoided if you use a scale room plan. First sketch the shape of the room on plain paper then, using a retractable tape measure, measure and mark all of the following on your rough plan: the length of walls and of any recesses, the width of doors or other openings, the size of windows and of radiators or other fixtures. Also include telephone sockets, power sockets and light switches. You can incorporate these in your master plan or draw up a separate electrical plan. Either way, it will greatly help your electrician. Now draw the plan up to scale on graph paper, using the symbols in my example. Include not only the door opening itself, but an indication of the way the door opens as this will affect where you put the furniture.

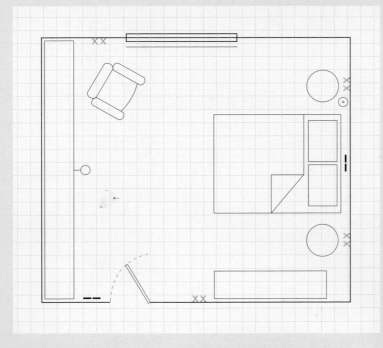

KEY TO DIAGRAM

TELEPHONE SOCKETS: It is always useful to have a telephone in the bedroom and, unless you have a cordless phone, it will require a socket.

POWER SOCKETS: One can never have too many of these. The National House Building Council recommends six in a main bedroom, four in other bedrooms.

PICTURE LIGHT: Illuminate the pictures on your bedroom wall with a picture light to complement your décor. Low-energy fittings are an option nowadays.

LIGHT SWITCHES: Locate light switches by the door, and near the bed. Dimmer switches make them more versatile and help enhance the mood.

THIS PAGE A neutral decorating scheme does not detract from the view over the gardens provided by floor-to-ceiling doors. A warm-coloured wooden floor completes the picture.

Drawing up a Schedule of Work

Whether you are simply redecorating your bedroom or are planning more major works, it pays to draw up a schedule of works so that essentials are not missed which will later require expensive remedy. I generally start with a Services and Structure checklist and then add a Decorating Schedule. You could also include a Furnishings Shopping List, giving the cost of each item and ticking it off as it is delivered. This can help you keep a check on your budget and on deliveries still to come. Finally, you can, if you wish, also draw up a chart showing which type of paint you want for walls, ceiling, woodwork and mouldings, which colour, how many coats and quantity required. Similarly, if you are using wallpaper, include number of rolls required.

SERVICES AND STRUCTURE

- Walls: remove any wallpaper; deal with cracks, leaks, damp; remove/install stud partition walls; repair cornices

- New services: install to 'first fix', i.e. wiring and pipework for plumbing and drainage for en-suite facilities, central heating, underfloor heating, air conditioning, electricity, ventilation, telephone sockets, home entertainment systems

- Floors: remove old floor coverings; check/strengthen floor joists if you want to install heavy flooring

- Doors and windows: check/repair door and window frames; check/repair window glass

- New services: install to 'second fix', i.e. fit sanitaryware, switches, lights, radiators, power sockets

- Joinery: fit built-in storage; fit new doors

- Floors and walls: lay hard flooring or sand floorboards; do tiling; fix skirting boards

DECORATING SCHEDULE

- Protect floors and furnishings

- Paint ceiling

- Undercoat all woodwork, doors, window frames, skirting boards

- Paint walls and cornices, or paper walls or hang with fabric if used

- Top coat woodwork

- Fix ironmongery

- Lay carpet

- Install window treatments

- Install light fittings

- Position furniture

- Add accessories

FURNISHINGS SHOPPING LIST

- Bed and headboard

- Mattress

- Flooring

- Lighting

- Window treatments

- Storage furniture

- Seating

- Tables

- Bedding

- Hardware

- Accessories

THIS PAGE In this rather romantic bedroom the headboard has a runner that can easily be removed for washing. The pretty pink and green colour scheme is fresh and light.

Decorative Options

Since bedrooms need impress no one except their owners, you can choose a style that is as personal and idiosyncratic as you like — as long as it is relaxing, comfortable and in no way jarring. But how to choose a style when there is so much choice? Elsie de Wolfe, the great American decorator of the 1920s and 1930s, had a mantra that went 'Suitability, Suitability, Suitability' and though this may sound dull and curbing to the imagination, it is actually sensible and certainly helps to whittle away the choices.

A great deal, as I have mentioned before, depends on the type of house or apartment you own, the climate where you live, the house's location, the size and proportions of the bedoom and your budget (see pages 28–31). Whether you happen to live in a new building or an old one, by the sea, deep in the country, in a suburb, in the heart of a city, in a hot climate or a cold one, and whether the room in question is a master bedroom, a child's room or a guest room, you will want to choose affordable things that will be appropriate to your surroundings as well as to the occupants of the room.

Another important factor may be what you already possess in terms of furniture, rugs and accessories. Unless you are starting from scratch, these will need to be taken into account. And in the same way, and most importantly if you are sharing the bedroom, whatever you choose must be acceptable to both of you.

TOP LEFT This sumptuously decorated en-suite bathroom features elaborate window treatments and paisley and carpet-covered pillows on the window seat.

TOP RIGHT Rough-hewn roof beams have been given a wash of pale grey paint for an updated country look.

CENTRE LEFT An urban, masculine bedroom features dark grey furnishings and accessories set against pale grey walls. The dark leather chair adds a period touch to the scheme.

CENTRE RIGHT Eclectic style often comprises things we have brought back from our travels, in this case, the bedroom has a mattress covered with crinkled Indian cotton standing on an Indian dhurrie.

BOTTOM LEFT A bold red curtain contrasts with the black, brass-buttoned bed and white bedlinen in an urban yet feminine bedroom.

BOTTOM RIGHT A mass of pillows in varying shades of white and delicate light fittings make this bedroom romantic rather than minimal.

MINIMAL

Minimalism is akin to size 0 models in the sense that the aim of minimalist designers is to create as sparsely furnished and accessoried a room as possible in order to show its 'bones'. This, as most normal families know, is next to impossible. Nevertheless, disciplined childless and single people can and do manage it, and so does the occasional family. A really contemplative zen-like minimal space can be charming and relaxing, but there is nothing, of course, to stop one also having a comfortable minimal space.

My dream minimal room would have mainly neutral, white, parchment, buff, grey or even black walls and flooring, and a crisply dressed skeletal metal or unadorned and uncurtained wooden four-poster bed. Bedside tables will be simple, there may be a chair or two, and a chest, chaise longue or couch at the end of the bed. Storage will be provided in the sleekest possible built-in cupboards. Lighting will consist of neat recessed ceiling lights and adjustable reading lamps built into the headboard, or there will be floor lamps either side of the bed. Windows will be shuttered or covered with plain blinds and there will generally be very little, if anything, in the way of pictures on the walls. All fabrics and materials will be totally fuss-free and there will be absolutely none of the clutter that one finds in less tightly controlled bedroom spaces.

LEFT Simplicity itself is the result in a converted Georgian cottage. The pale grey colour scheme is restful and the room contains only the bare essentials for a bedroom – a bed, a small bedside table and some fitted cupboards.

OPPOSITE In this bedroom in South Africa, the only adornment is the display recess in the wall and the black-and-white rugs on the floor. The bedside tables are as understated as they could possibly be. Even the bedspread weave is hardly there.

A SPARE AND AESTHETIC LOOK CAN BE
WONDERFULLY CALMING TO THE SPIRIT BUT
IT REQUIRES MUCH DISCIPLINE, RESOLUTE
TIDINESS, AND MAXIMUM STORAGE

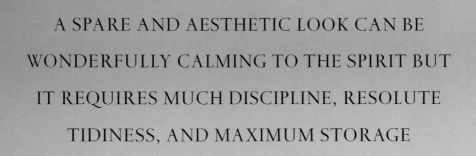

ROMANTIC

There are many versions of the romantic style but soft and feminine are key words. Delicate colouring is provided by paint, paper or fabric-covered walls, by sheer fabrics at the windows and by beautifully dressed, seductive-looking beds. Floor coverings, whether fitted carpeting or rugs, are soft to the feet. Lighting is ultra-soft, often with rose-coloured silk-lined lampshades to create a mellow glow, and seating is comfortable and cushioned. Accessories are *de rigueur* — silver-framed photographs, cut-glass perfume bottles and bowls on lace tablecloths or on old embroidered white linen or broderie anglaise. The finishing touches are bowls of sweet-smelling potpourri or vases of flowers, and charming prints on the walls.

ABOVE A deep eighteenth-century crocheted lace valance forms the finishing touch to a draped linen curtain caught back against the wall alongside the bed. This charmingly romantic American bedroom looks out over a well-planted terrace.

RIGHT Aubergine-coloured toile de Jouy provides the romantic element in this bedroom. It is offset by the crisp white bedding and a painted Gustavian-style chest of drawers.

OPPOSITE Softly coloured pattern on chair and quilt are here teamed with a small check cotton bedcover, a self-check voile bed canopy and pristine lace-trimmed pillows.

THIS PAGE Here, an evidently comfortably upholstered and seductive-looking bed is set in front of windows hung with simple pure silk curtains. The two accent colours are the pure white bedlinen and the gingery dried hydrangea heads.

OPPOSITE BELOW The lavish use of textiles on every possible surface does much to create a sumptuous bedroom look. This room is furnished to be as much luxurious boudoir as bedroom.

SUMPTUOUS

If you yearn for the sumptuous look then you are a real luxury-lover and you will need to have a budget to match. A sumptuous bedroom, whether traditional or of the more pared-down contemporary variety, is invariably costly and it is *meant* to look as if no expense has been spared. You want the most handsome furniture you can find, and it should be top-quality. For dressing the bed and windows, look for enveloping fabrics, with the emphasis on real silks and silk velvets. For the floor, for preference choose deep-pile carpet, antique floorboards and old rugs, or, in hot climates, luxurious marble or granite. Ambient lighting should be subtle and concealed, perhaps behind a false ceiling. You may want fabric-covered walls and the bed needs to be made to look as seductive and inviting as possible. Stunning flowers and plants complete the picture.

URBAN

Urban style, where bedrooms are concerned, immediately conjures up words associated with city elegance such as sophistication, tailoring and, more and more these days, a particular type of masculine discrimination. Such urban or, one might say, urbane, chic, often entails luxurious fitted carpeting or dark polished-wood floors with Oriental or other sumptuous rugs on top, or – the complete opposite – contemporary polished or resin-topped concrete or smoothly gleaming stone.

On the walls, one might find rich wood panelling, deeply gleaming lacquer, or sometimes heavy fabric. Window treatments are kept crisp and rather tailored with roman blinds, roller blinds or venetian blinds in wood or metal. Sometimes you might find neat shutters or simple curtains in plain colours or bold designs. Whatever the choice, the key word is uncluttered.

BELOW LEFT A polished floor, cement plaster walls, the low table made of a piece of antique cedar and the strong horizontals created by the two shelves give a sturdy feel to this studio apartment. Note the division the rug makes between the bedroom and the living space.

BELOW This urban bedroom has an Oriental feel that comes from the panels of woven wood covering the walls. The furniture is rather austere, though the red armchair and footstool add a surprising note.

Furniture, whether antique or modern, tends to be of good quality and the best of its kind, and a great deal of attention is usually paid to good, well-organized storage furniture where, as they say, there is a place for everything and everything is in its place.

Urban colours of choice range from camels and greys, chestnut browns and reds, to dark greens and navy, and even to black, while favoured fabrics are those such as men's suiting, felts, flannels, smooth tweeds, corduroys, close-woven velvety wools and smooth dark velvets. These rather masculine fabrics can just as easily be used on the walls as for the upholstery. If pattern is used, the sophisticated urbanite will favour stripes, checks and graphic prints. And any art, accessories and plants used as finishing touches will invariably have been chosen with a discriminating eye.

ABOVE This very masculine bedroom with its walls in bone-coloured faux suede has a black leather bed dressed with black-and-white bedlinen. The bedside tables are in dark rosewood and there are adjustable chrome reading lights. The graphic print on the wall picks up on the graphic quality of the rest of the room.

RIGHT Different striped fabrics and an interesting cream-and-grey toile de Jouy for the half-tester allied to contrasting walls make this a beguiling urban-style bedroom. The small chest of drawers by the bed is practical.

OPPOSITE In this bedroom, interestingly finished walls provide a backdrop to a sunburst mirror whose rays pick up the colour of the rich green curtains and of the lamp bases. Zebra-striped cushions echo the zig-zag border on the headboard and valance and the chairs are upholstered, rather unexpectedly, in pale chintz, which lends a more feminine air to the room.

THIS PAGE Here, wooden panels form the doors of wall-to-wall clothes storage that 'floats' above floor level. The wall above the bed is partially clad in dramatically grained wood with a built-in shelf to match. The circles on the retro-style bedspread are repeated on the rug.

RIGHT An early nineteenth-century coaching inn in Normandy has had its A-frame roof beams exposed to full view. The muted colours of the room are gently relaxing and are the perfect foil to the somewhat grand painting above the bed. The upholstered stool at the foot of the bed adds a somewhat unexpected contemporary touch.

ABOVE The exterior wall of this pretty country-style bedroom in Connecticut is of stone, but the effect is light and airy, thanks to the limed wood-plank interior walls and beamed ceiling, the good natural light and the white bedding. A group of eight pressed flower pictures are in keeping with the room and form a visual extension to the beige headboard.

COUNTRY

Country styles differ somewhat from country to country and range from the deliberately rustic to the sophisticatedly flowery. It is good to remember though, that although it is perfectly acceptable to practise a country look in town – the *rus in urbe* of ancient Rome – it is not nearly as suitable to make an urban-looking bedroom in the country.

English Country style is characterized by good mahogany and/or painted furniture on polished floorboards or carpet with perhaps some beautiful *gros point* rugs on top. The bed will often have an imposing headboard or may be a four-poster and will be made of brass, iron or carved wood. Fabrics are a comfortable mix of botanical and bird prints on cotton or glazed chintz.

American Country style might well feature centre-stage a Colonial post bed with an old (or maybe home-made) patchwork quilt, in a traditional

ABOVE This bedroom is in Adirondack style and the headboard and footboard have been constructed from the branches of fallen trees from the grounds of the house. The country theme continues with a European touch: the bedspread and cushions are Hungarian, with a black-and-white peasant-style pattern.

American design. Polished wooden floorboards are common and are sometimes stencilled, this being a popular decorative effect used by people who could not afford or did not want carpets. To soften the bare floorboards, try some cosy-looking rag rugs and put airy lace curtains at the windows. If you have eighteenth- or nineteenth-century shutters, flaunt them. They are naturally at home with this look. For furniture, choose distressed painted or pine. A wooden rocking chair would be especially appropriate, as would naïve portraits or landscapes on the walls.

French Country style ranges from the colourful Provençal look, with brightly coloured printed and woven fabrics with small-scale patterns in primary and secondary colours, to the more sophisticated and subtle look of toile de Jouy whose designs can be found on both wallpaper and fabric.

OPPOSITE ABOVE In this log cabin on a hillside in New Mexico, the wood theme of the walls is continued with a four-poster bed with a carved wooden headboard draped with white linen.

OPPOSITE BELOW Here the totally different country look in a guest bedroom comes from simple coordinated striped, sprigged and checked cottons, plain white walls, an antique iron bedstead and dainty flower prints on the wall.

RIGHT This sleeping loft enjoys spectacular views of the mountains. A Native American throw and animal skins decorate the bed, while a kayak hanging above helps continue the outdoors-in theme.

Traditional toile de Jouy colours are blue and white, green and white, red and white, rose and white, grey and white or black and white, all of which look charming in a small bedroom with a mixture of pine, cane or painted furniture. In a larger bedroom there is scope to mix toile de Jouy with gingham or stripes, or with small florals in the same tones.

Rustic style, often called Cabin style in the United States, harks back to that country's rugged pioneering spirit of old. It features beamed walls and ceilings, walls of old brick or stone, walls covered with tongue-and-groove planks of wood or with, simply, rough, unhewn planks. The wood is always left unpainted and may be complemented by wide unpolished floorboards with rugs, by floors of brick, stone or quarry tiles, or by floor coverings of sisal or rush matting. Window treatments are normally simple cotton curtains, plain blinds or wooden shutters. Furniture looks rustic, even hand-hewn and bed frames and headboards might be made of unfinished timber, even of rough branches and twigs. Another option is a simple antique-style iron bed frame. Bedlinen will be spankingly white, but might well be topped by a plaid bedspread or quilt, or by a homespun-cover or Native American piece of weaving.

THIS PAGE Painted oval landscapes on canvas are here used as a backdrop-cum-headboard. Teamed with a totally disparate bedspread, tablecloth and throw, it looks interesting rather than in any way ill-considered.

ABOVE This bedroom, with its objects and artefacts collected from all around the world, reflects its travel-loving owners. The green bedcover, intricate screen and paintings stand out against the mainly white bed that is flanked by a tailored white cloth-covered table and white chair set on a white floor.

ABOVE RIGHT A metal-framed glass wall and door (with curtains for privacy) screen a pale green bedroom with interestingly chosen furniture and furnishings and a dramatic bedspread and skin rug.

ECLECTIC

Eclectic style, a term that is sometimes used as an expression of contempt, is what many of us have willy-nilly. That is to say it is a mixture. It can be quite undeliberate, in which case it may be the result of combining things we have already, or it can simply comprise things that we like for no particular reason. Another possibility is that it is deliberate, for example the deliberate mixture of the old and the new, such as a heavy seventeenth-century oak chest combined with a stark metal bed and with contemporary abstract paintings. Or it can be a mixture of the frivolous and the serious, the sentimental and the prized, the naïve and the sophisticated. Whatever sort of mixture you have, bring it all together via an all-embracing common theme, whether of colour, pattern or fabric. For example, try the same pattern on the walls as for the bedcover, headboard, curtains or blinds, or unite the bedroom's disparate elements with neutral sisal flooring.

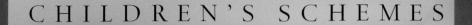

CHILDREN'S SCHEMES

Many first-time parents are apt to spend money on furniture and accoutrements for the first year or two of a child's life which are actually more gratifying for themselves than for the child. The basic needs for a small child's bedroom are versatile lighting that can be turned right down to a glow if the child is frightened of the dark; a cosy, comforting environment; suitable furniture for clothes and toy storage; and every possible attention to safety.

SAFETY FIRST

You may think you have anticipated every danger, but it is surprising what crawling babies and toddlers can get up to in the way of pushing their fingers into power sockets or climbing up things you never would have imagined they could, and then gaily launching themselves off, or worse, falling out of windows. So the first rule is to ensure that all power sockets are recessed flush with the wall and, if possible, that they are placed higher than normal to be out of reach for the child. Fit covers over unused sockets, too.

Keep all electrical appliances and lamps well out of reach and see that there are no trailing cables for a child to trip over, pull, or, heaven forbid, get entangled with. Make sure that fireplaces, stoves, oil-filled or electric heaters and fans are well guarded, and always fit a safety gate at the door of the bedroom and at the top and bottom of any stairs.

THIS PAGE In this child's room, patchwork-style bedspreads edged with tiny checked cotton look quite classic on the limed-wood beds. The beds are full size so they will not be quickly outgrown, while the bedding can be easily replaced as the children get older.

OPPOSITE A charmingly papered mini chest of drawers is here used as a bedside table and picks up the apple green of the blanket as well as the blue-grey of the imposing double doors.

If the child's bedroom is located higher than the first or ground floor of the building, fit either window locks or vertical bars to prevent the child from climbing out. Such window bars should be spaced no more than 12.5cm (5in) apart and certainly not wide enough apart for a child to get his or her head stuck through. If you think they look too prison-like, you can always paint them in a cheerful colour.

It is also important, both for yourself and for the child, to have a non-slip floor in the bedroom. Carpet or cork are good choices as they are comfortable to crawl on yet suitable for the child to play on easily with wheeled toys. Cork can even be painted for a game of hopscotch or with roads marked for toy cars.

Try also to ensure that no surface is high enough to be a source of danger to a child with a sense of exploration and a predilection for climbing, nor that there are any hard, sharp objects or sharp corners of furniture anywhere in the bedroom. And finally, make sure that drawers cannot easily be pulled out and used as steps for inquisitive small people, nor that they can be pulled right out so they fall on and injure the child.

THE ROOM THAT GROWS WITH THE CHILD
If you want to have an eye for the future, stick to simple, sturdy and classic decoration for a child's room, and ensure the room has adequate switches and power sockets from the outset, to cope with all the lighting,

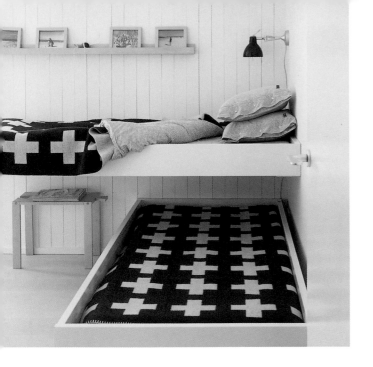

entertainment and computing requirements that may be needed as the child gets older. You should also avoid special child-sized furniture that the child will outgrow in a few years. Follow these simple pointers and you will have a room that can be kept roughly as it is for many years, from the child's infancy to its teens. All that will be needed as the child grows will be simple changes, for instance from crib to cot to twin beds or bunk beds (for sleepovers or for a second child), from toy and infant clothes cupboards to full-length wardrobes, from play space to homework space, and from baby décor to décor that will be more in keeping with a toddler, then a school child, and finally a teenager. None of this need incur undue expense nor involve great disruption.

ABOVE Built-in bunk beds at right angles have bold bedcovers in different colourways.

OPPOSITE FAR LEFT This sturdy wooden bed is inviting for a child and would not be grown out of too quickly.

OPPOSITE LEFT A dark wood Norwegian log cabin of 1925 has its original furniture, including an unusual pair of bunk beds with exceptionally elegant barley-sugar twist legs.

RIGHT This neat pair of white-painted bunk beds has a useful cupboard beneath. With its crisp blue-and-white decoration, the room will long outlast the children's early years.

THIS PAGE Blue-and-white bedrooms are always a refreshing sight. In this guest bedroom, the patchwork-style quilt and coordinating cushions and pillows, the blue-edged lampshades and the blue-trimmed roman blind look beguiling and fresh.

- A comfortable chair will make your guest feel relaxed and at home.

- Include a generous bedside table with a selection of reading matter, some bottled water and a tin of biscuits.

- Your guest needs a place for clothes. If there is not room for a cupboard, provide some hooks on the wall or on the back of the door, or a hat stand or towel rail.

- Privacy is a must for a guest, so make sure the door has a lock that works.

Guest Rooms

Guest bedrooms should be as comfortable as they are interestingly decorated. Sadly, whatever mattress you choose cannot suit everybody but you can make up for this by offering a choice of firm or soft, and feather or synthetic pillows as well as the best bedlinen you can. In the interests of privacy and for guests who abhor early-morning light, ensure that you have well-fitting, lined curtains at the windows and perhaps even light-excluding blinds. Good ventilation is a must, together with adequate heating in winter and air-conditioning or at least a fan in summer. For chilly nights an electric blanket will be appreciated. And as well as good ambient light, provide a bedside light for reading in bed and a good light for shaving or putting on make-up.

ABOVE It goes without saying that a comfortable chair in a guest room is always a bonus. This one blends in gently with walls and bed.

RIGHT Rose-coloured walls, curtains and valance, not to mention the rose-coloured lamp bases and trim of the bedlinen, are designed to give a welcoming glow to a guest bedroom.

LIGHT AND AIRY

If you are lucky enough to have a light and airy room, make the most of it. If not, you can still give the impression that you have one. I, for example, once had a bedroom with chocolate-coloured walls but with a white ceiling, white woodwork and palest cream carpet and bedcover. Despite the dark walls, people seeing the room invariably came away with an impression of light.

The trick lies in ensuring that large areas of the room should be in colours taken from the white, pale neutral or pale pastel palette of colours. Pale floors and a pale ceiling are a must, but pale woodwork, furniture and accessories will help to underline the pale theme.

To maintain the sense of light and air, keep the window treatments, bed dressing, upholstery and cushions light and minimal, choosing, for preference, cottons, voiles and batistes. Nor should you forget the power of white-painted shutters, pale-coloured slatted blinds or sliding fabric panels to add to the impression of a luminous airiness.

Furniture should be chosen for its lightness of construction and you could consider see-through tables and chairs in Perspex or Plexiglass. Another option is to have some surfaces in the bedroom, such as mirror, glass and silver, that catch, reflect and exaggerate both daylight and artificial light.

LUMINOUS, LIGHT-FILLED BEDROOMS BRING A SENSE OF WELL-BEING AND PLEASURE, ESPECIALLY TO THOSE OF US WHO ARE OBLIGED TO LIVE WITHIN THE CONFINES OF TODAY'S FAST-PACED URBAN ENVIRONMENTS

THIS PAGE Very often, the deliberate injection of an opposing element in a room serves to exaggerate some aspect. In this case, the dark upholstery of the chair underlines the room's whiteness.

OPPOSITE The chandelier, understated white four-poster bed, white rugs, white floor and the upholstered seat at the foot of the bed all serve to enhance the feeling of light and air in this simple yet elegant bedroom.

DARK AND COSY

This sophisticated look with its rather masculine air perhaps suits the confines of the bedroom better than it would the more public areas of the home. It might be the choice of those who dislike early-morning sun and it certainly looks effective by lamplight. Inevitably, dark colours prevail, the most chic of which are black, greys and browns, all of which can be accompanied by a wide range of contrasting colours. Pictures and ornaments provide further contrast, like a gallery where every piece on display has maximum impact. The sense of enclosure can be greatly enhanced by the choice of soft-textured fabrics such as silks and velvets, chenilles, wools and furs, or even the softer tweeds, while the ultimate in bedroom cosiness is to have upholstered walls. Not only do these look as luxurious as they feel, but they have the advantage of deadening obtrusive sounds and making the bedroom feel even more womb-like. You may want to complete the dark and cosy effect with light-excluding window treatments, the ultimate of which are blackout blinds or curtains with blackout linings.

OPPOSITE The dark soft-looking but tailored bed with the tweed throw contrasts with the curved, brass-studded leather chair and angled lamps.

BELOW A collection of plaster medallions and prints stands out against the grey walls as do the white-painted chair and antique bedcover.

BELOW LEFT This bed, with its tall dark leather headboard and sturdy wooden posts is balanced by the dark wood floor and the campaign chests.

UNEXPECTED

Since bedrooms are the part of the home where you need impress no one but yourself, they offer you the chance to indulge in a colour scheme or decorating theme that you would not necessarily want to use in more public areas. Thus you might find a bedroom that is unusually sumptuous compared to other rooms in the house, or one that is unexpectedly monastic, where the rest of the home is rather plush and comfortable. The unexpected in bedrooms can range from fanciful to fantasy, they can bedazzle with knock-you-in-the-eye primary colours, or they can be decorated from top to bottom in bleached-out white.

I have seen bedrooms designed like tents and others with so many padded surfaces that they feel to me like a claustrophobic tunnel. Then there are bedrooms like ship's cabins that are all polished wood built-in storage with matching built-in bed; bedrooms with walls bedecked with necklaces, lace, mirrors and fans; and even bedrooms made to resemble a golf course, complete with Astroturf 'carpeting' punctuated by holes to practise one's putting. Anything can go.

THIS PAGE A dramatic padded head- and footboard ensure that this bed takes centre stage. The lines of the quilting stand out in sharp contrast to the white walls, while simple chrome-and-glass bedside tables do not detract from the bedroom's bold simplicity.

All About the Bed

It may seem a statement of the obvious, but a bedroom is just as much about the bed as a dining room is about the dining table. If the bed and mattress are not comfortable, then no amount of beautiful decoration and bed dressing will make up for that fact. The first step, then, is to get to know as much as possible about beds and mattresses — what makes a stylish bed choice, what space-saving beds are available, what the differences are between the vast array of mattresses on the high street and what shapes and sizes do they come in? Where you position the bed in the room may seem obvious, but some surprising lateral thinking can help to make your bedroom space work better.

Headboards have quite an impact in the room, so choosing one is another important decision you need to face. I show and discuss a wide range of possibilities. Only then is it time to look at the other elements that will make your sleeping hours comfortable, from pillows, duvets and bedlinen to old-fashioned blankets, comforters and eiderdowns. And finally, there are the purely decorative elements that you might wish to add, such as cushions, throws, drapes and hangings. These will help to add the finishing touches. I explore which are the best fabrics to use and how to give the bed a tailored or flouncy, romantic or minimal look. Combine these many elements and you will be on your way to a good and stylish night's sleep.

TOP LEFT Stitched and padded quilts of Indian cotton are complemented by a cluster of silk and gold-thread cushions set against an enormous padded and buttoned corner headboard.

TOP RIGHT Red-and-white toile de Jouy hung from a pole forms a classic canopy over a handsome sleigh bed. The same fabric covers the bolster and quilt.

CENTRE LEFT Pale primrose and soft green fringed throws will add a touch of comfort to the bed during the cold winter months.

CENTRE RIGHT An almost plain white sheet is complemented by a double-sided blue-and-white bedspread for a cool summer look.

BOTTOM LEFT If you are on a budget, painted floorboards and second-hand painted furniture leave you money to spare for lavish broderie anglaise-trimmed bedlinen and a luxurious wool blanket.

BOTTOM RIGHT The white iron bedstead, white sheets and gauzy bed curtains are in marked contrast to the dark embroidered bedcover.

CHOOSING A BED

Go out shopping to buy a bed and before you even start to think about the perplexing range of mattress types and sizes – of which more later on pages 84–85 – you will be faced with an enormous choice of styles of bed frames made in an equally enormous range of materials. Would you like an antique bed or a reproduction – with the look of an old bed but worm-

and rust-free? Do you favour the shape of a sleigh bed or *lit bateau*, or one of the other types of bed with an integral head- and footboard? Or maybe you would infinitely prefer the neat look of a divan bed with a tailored bedspread and valance and a separate tall padded headboard. Or perhaps you have always craved for one of those appealing Victorian or Edwardian brass

OPPOSITE FAR LEFT A handsome carved and turned-wood Colonial bed with its four sculptural pillars is paired here with 1930s bedside tables and swing-arm wall lamps that are perfect for bedtime reading. Crisp white bedlinen makes a beautiful contrast.

OPPOSITE TOP LEFT This handsome carved and canopied Oriental piece is as perfect for a bed as it is for relaxed seating.

OPPOSITE BELOW LEFT The tent-like canopy over this four-poster bed reflects the shape of the ceiling above.

RIGHT A contemporary low bed with unobtrusive side tables is influenced by pared-down Japanese decorating style.

or iron bedsteads or a carved wooden bedstead of the same era. Then again, perhaps you would only choose a contemporary bed, in which case look at the many on the market that have only the simplest, most minimal of frames, often on slim, tapered legs and often rather low to the ground. These beds are best suited to the uncluttered loft-style or Japanese-style bedrooms that are so popular nowadays.

At the other extreme, many people love four-poster beds, or charming American Colonial beds which are similar in that they have four wooden posts but without the top rails. For a more up-to-date look,

there are modern equivalents made in elegant steel or stark wrought iron. Perhaps the idea of a fabric approximation of a four-poster bed appeals to you. If so, turn to pages 86–87 to see how to make one yourself.

MORE THAN A BED

Quite apart from the usual rectangular beds you can also find round beds, heart-shaped beds and square beds. In fact, you can order a bed in any shape you fancy, but do not forget that wayward shapes will need specially made bedlinens. And if unusually shaped beds are not enough to whet your appetite, nowadays you can also find beds with electronic controls to raise the head or foot of the bed to suit the occupier's fancy, beds with integral television in the footboard or beds with a clock and stereo in the headboard. Then there are also beds with integral bedside tables, bookshelves and lighting. The possibilities are endless.

SPACE-SAVING BEDS

If you are short of space or have a studio apartment or dual-purpose room, then take a look at a Murphy bed, which folds up against the wall and into a cupboard if you wish. It is raised and lowered thanks to a spring-loaded counter-balancing system. Then there are sofa beds and sofa chairs which are also especially suitable for studio apartments or for dual-purpose rooms, providing you with a spare bed for occasional guests.

We do not all have room for a pair of twin beds, but again, there are many space-saving options on the market. The most common is perhaps the bunk bed, which is most suitable for children, though not for very tiny tots. Bunk beds come in styles ranging from the very simplest to much more elaborate creations which are as much play frame as bed. You can also find bunk beds that can be taken apart when the children are older to become a pair of single beds, and if saving space is a priority, there are even bunk beds that fold flat against the wall when not in use, rather like the Murphy bed.

Another space-saving solution when a pair of beds is needed for occasional use is the single bed that conceals another bed and mattress underneath. The lower one is fitted with castors and has spring-loaded legs that bring it up to full height.

LEFT This elegant nineteenth-century iron bedstead is happily decked out with patchwork cushions and a two-tone bedspread.

OPPOSITE TOP LEFT For a calming effect, an eighteenth-century four-poster is lavishly hung with a hand-embroidered linen lined with pale green silk.

OPPOSITE TOP RIGHT With a padded screen acting as a headboard, this comfortable-looking mattress covered with a cosy diamond-patterned quilt is in stark contrast to the stone-clad base on which it stands.

OPPOSITE BELOW LEFT An old wooden Norwegian 'heaven' bed is so-called because the sleeper feels protected by it. It feels like a snug room-within-a-room and is perfect for long Scandinavian winter nights. Storage space beneath makes it an even more practical addition to a bedroom.

OPPOSITE BELOW RIGHT Cheerfully dressed bunk beds are perfect for children and fit just so between tongue-and-groove walls and a capacious chest of drawers. Utilitarian wall lamps echo the metal drawer handles.

OPPOSITE Simple futon mattresses are placed straight onto tatami matting and are shielded by shoji screens in a Japanese-inspired bedroom.

BELOW The intricate coil springs of a yet-to-be covered sprung mattress.

BELOW RIGHT A covered and buttoned mattress gives the sleeper firm support on top of a metal bed frame.

MATTRESS CHOICES

A good mattress should give you at least a decade or so of comfortable use and with care, several more years after that. The main mattress sizes are as follows: a standard single is 90cm (3ft) x 190cm (6ft 3in); a small double is 135cm (4ft 6in) x 190cm (6ft 3in); a standard double (sometimes called a Queen) is 150cm (5ft) x 200cm (6ft 6in); an American Queen is 170cm (5ft 6in) x 215cm (7ft); a King is 180cm (6ft) x 215cm (7ft); a Californian King which is 200cm (6ft 6in) x 230cm (7ft 6in).

There are two main kinds of mattress – foam and sprung. The foam type are made from polyurethane or latex rubber. Sprung mattresses can either have pocketed or the less expensive open springs. Pocketed springs are each sewn into their own pocket and so are unaffected by the compression of neighbouring springs. They are therefore particularly desirable for beds used by couples of widely differing weights. Open springs consist of a network of hour-glass springs. These mattresses are more common.

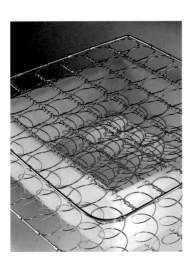

THIS PAGE Narrow, trimmed branches are attached to each other to form a rustic four-poster that is hung with lightweight fabric attached by ties. Tall, narrow twigs makes an equally arresting bedhead.

- Fix four timber battens directly above the bed to the ceiling to make a frame that is slightly bigger than the made-up bed.

- Fix a length of Velcro to each corner of the frame and stitch the other face of the Velcro pieces to the top of four lengths of hemmed fabric, long enough to hang from the frame and 'puddle' on the floor.

- Fix a tailored or gathered pelmet or ruffle to the battens to finish it off and conceal the top of the curtains.

Make Your Own Four-Poster

Four-poster beds are making a comeback, though gone are the days when draught-proofing was their purpose. Nowadays people choose the four-poster look for aesthetic reasons. There is no longer a need for heavy velvet or brocade drapes. Instead look at the ranges of lightweight sheers, linens and cottons. Some bedding ranges also include fabric by the metre which you can use for the drapes of your bed to give a totally coordinated look if you choose. Gone, too, are the ornately carved wooden frames of yesteryear's four-posters. Today's frames can just as easily be made from simple wooden beams or metal poles. If you do not need your bed curtains to close, the frame can even consist of nothing more than battens fixed to the ceiling.

ABOVE This simple and sculptural white-painted wooden four-poster needs nothing more than a tailored muslin valance to top it off.

RIGHT Another starkly simple wooden four-poster has a headboard resembling a garden bench. The effect is softened somewhat by the gathered hanging and the various cushions.

THIS PAGE This comfortable-looking bed is beautifully positioned alongside sliding glass doors that lead out to a cool screened terrace surrounded by tropical greenery.

POSITIONING

THE BED

Practitioners of Feng Shui have plenty to say about the best position for a bed but mostly, if rooms are only of small to average size, one has a very limited choice. The result is that the bed has to be placed wherever seems most practical in relation to, say, a wall of cupboards or a fireplace, or in order, for example, to avoid a window with a radiator beneath. If you want to be able to watch television in bed, that might determine where you position the bed, or you may want to position it in such a way as to be able to take advantage of a beautiful view from the window.

This effectively means that the majority of people position their bed in the centre of a wall, with the bedhead up against the wall. This usually ensures that there is room around the bed for a pair of bedside tables as well as space to make the bed easily without having to sidle around it. If you have a small bedroom and a double bed, which renders this arrangement impossible, you may have to position the bed lengthways against the wall, which generally means an ungainly crawl across the bed for the person sleeping on the wall side.

But if the size of the room is not a particular problem, there is no reason why a bed cannot be placed right in the middle of the room. This can produce a stunning room-dividing effect, which can be further enhanced by using an extra tall headboard (see pages 90–93), a headboard that incorporates side tables and storage, or even a headboard that is actually a tall cupboard, accessed from behind the bed. In a bedroom with en-suite facilities, the tall headboard could even conceal a shower and washbasin if you wish.

HEADBOARDS

If total comfort in bed is of paramount importance, then that search for comfort will affect your choice of headboard. Headboards come in all shapes and sizes and can be made of a multitude of different materials, from traditional wood or metal to those that are just token headboards, made from a length of fabric draped behind the head of the bed. Such token headboards do not really add much to the sum of comfort for the bed. However, there is a feeling now for oversized, very tall and upholstered headboards, some almost as tall as the bed is long.

While a soft, upholstered headboard is desirable, always look for a fabric that is spongeable or can be readily cleaned with an upholstery cleaner. Soft headboards can get quite unexpectedly grubby from the heads constantly

ABOVE Large, quilted squares on a dark headboard are matched in proportion by the black bedside table and in comfort by the luxurious-looking duvet with its spanking white cotton cover.

RIGHT An elaborately carved late nineteenth-century wood-and-fabric screen serves as an oversized headboard, and is complemented by an equally elaborate bedspread in this idiosyncratic bedroom.

OPPOSITE A towering upholstered berry-coloured headboard with matching valance is offset by an even taller mirror propped up against the wall. A sleek metal table and elaborate lamp that looks like an ecclesiastical candlestick complete the scheme.

pressed up against them. An inexpensive alternative to a lavish upholstered headboard is to use slip-covered foam slung from poles attached to the wall behind the bed. The covers can easily be removed for cleaning.

If looks and originality are more important to you than comfort, then there appears to be practically no limit to what you can use as a headboard. I have seen screens of every description used, not to mention tapestries, rugs and large paintings. I have even seen one headboard made of very realistic faux box trees and another that consisted of an ornamental trellis complete with climbing plants.

Many contemporary understated headboards may not offer much in the way of comfort, but they are often very practical since they might incorporate bedside tables and lamps, a useful shelf or two for books or ornaments, or even a pair of speakers to lull you to sleep with your favourite music. The ultimate modern headboard is the room-divider headboard (see page 89), which is so large that you can walk around it.

HEADBOARDS CAN RANGE FROM FRIVOLOUS TO PRAGMATIC, FROM LUXURIOUS TO FRANKLY CURIOUS, FROM TAILORED TO FANTASTICAL – IT ALL DEPENDS ON YOUR TASTE, COMFORT AND BUDGET

OPPOSITE ABOVE LEFT Since the sloping walls in this attic bedroom made it impossible to have a regular headboard, the owners created the illusion of one by draping a fabric panel from a roof beam.

OPPOSITE ABOVE RIGHT Twin beds have neat headboards made from buttoned and quilted material hung from rails fixed to the wall above. This cost-cutting idea can easily be made at home.

LEFT This pretty child's bedroom has a leaf-shaped headboard made from firm foam to add an element of fun to the room. Note how the bed itself is, by contrast, quite tailored.

RIGHT ABOVE This formidable winged headboard is very like a large version of some airline seats. Combined with the varied textures of the bedcovers, it makes the bedroom look very tactile. Note the practical, well-situated swing-arm lamps for bedside reading.

RIGHT The wonderfully scribed look of this fabric-covered headboard provides an airy-looking contrast to the heavier, distinctive check of the fabric used for the valance and to cover the bench at the foot of the bed. The colour scheme is in gentle tones of mushroom, beige and bluish lilac.

DRESSING THE BED

Since there is no ignoring the bed in a bedroom, how you dress it will clearly set the tone for the whole room. Fortunately, there has never been a better choice of bedlinen than there is now, whether you are looking for basic items such as flat or fitted sheets, duvet covers, valances and pillowcases, or extras like cushions and throws, quilts and comforters or drapes and hangings. Not only do manufacturers now offer every conceivable permutation of colour, trim, pattern and thread count, but many produce ranges of coordinating bedlinen, throws and curtains that take the pain out of achieving the look you desire.

The classic choices for sheets and duvet covers, are Egyptian cotton, which looks crisp and cool, and linen, which is more expensive but feels luxurious and soft. If you are not a convert to duvets – those filled with goose down are the best, while hollow fibre are the budget option – then look at lambswool, mohair or even cashmere blankets, or a mix of fibres. Although sheets and blankets involve more work than simply throwing a duvet over the bed, the result is a more tailored look.

If the excess of choice that is available for dressing your bed fills you with bewilderment, I feel a certain sympathy, but read on and be inspired.

PILLOWS

Pillows can make or break your night's sleep. Some of us cannot sleep without a good down pillow, while others prefer the firmer man-made fibre pillows or simply have an allergy to down. In fact, so varied are people's pillow requirements, that good hotels now give their guests a choice of pillows, which is a sensible example to follow for your own overnight guests.

Whether they are of fibre or feathers, pillows come in a great variety of qualities at commensurate prices. If you are not sure which type of pillow type is best for you – which aligns your head and neck best, and which is correct for your preferred sleeping position – there are a few facts you need to know. Side sleepers require the firm support that synthetic or very highly stuffed pillows provide; medium pillows, such as those filled with soft down or soft synthetic are best for back sleepers, while stomach sleepers require soft pillows such as the softest down. If you are shopping for down, check the 'fill power' (the volume of space that 30g/1oz of down takes up). The higher the fill power, the better the pillow's resilience. Goose down is the best; it can last from five to ten years, while synthetic pillows will last one to two years. Pillows should always be covered with a pillowcase of the tightest-weave Egyptian or Pima cotton or cotton percale that you can afford.

THIS PAGE This neutral colour scheme, whose tone is set by the cream-painted wooden walls and oversized headboard, is carried through on the bed with its pile of cushions and windowpane-check coverlet.

OPPOSITE In this bedroom, firm, crisp cotton-covered pillows are neatly piled at the top of the bed and there is a simple grey-edged cover.

OPPOSITE FAR LEFT
A sumptuous mixture of silk, satin and velvet pillows in shades of green enliven an off-white bedcover.

OPPOSITE LEFT Blue and white always look fresh on a bed. Here a mixture of plaids, plains and sprigged florals are picture-perfect.

OPPOSITE BELOW LEFT
A Spanish embroidered shawl looks enticingly mysterious through the sheer curtains of this charming four-poster bed.

OPPOSITE BELOW RIGHT
A casual country look is achieved here by a mélange of cushions and bolsters with a faded cotton trellis-print quilt.

BELOW LEFT The crisp nautical look of blue-and-white ticking is softened by the addition of a broderie anglaise pillow.

BELOW RIGHT Dark, exotic tones prevail with rose and gold cushions in different sizes, a charcoal grey silk-covered bolster and a rose and blue striped throw, all piled on top of an iron daybed.

CUSHIONS AND THROWS

If you want to add some comfort as well as an extra decorative and even exotic dimension to the bedroom, including some cushions and throws is one way to do it. Layer them on the bed as well as on armchairs, daybeds, chaises and stools. They come in such a wide range of fabrics that it is easy to indulge a fantasy, whether that is to create a cocoon-like bedroom with cushions and throws in wool, angora, cashmere, pashmina and faux fur; a crisp effect with cotton and linen; a boudoir look with embroidery, velvet and dévoré; or a country-house ambience with floral prints complemented by plains. Pull a throw over you for a quick siesta or as an extra layer on a cold night. Comfort your back against a pile of welcoming cushions. One way and another cushions and throws are always a great adjunct to a bedroom.

DRAPES AND HANGINGS

In this eclectic era many styles of bed draperies, curtains, hangings and canopies are to be seen. It is hardly surprising that they are perennially popular: the imaginative use of fabric is the quickest and often the most cost-effective way to glamorize a bed. Using fabric you can create the grandest of beds or the simply graceful. You can have a full-blown four-poster complete with back hangings, contrast curtain linings and sunburst pleating for the 'ceiling', or you can simply drape fabric so that it falls behind the bed or at either side. Achieve these simpler effects by using one or more poles fitted with finials, by hanging the fabric from a canopy or half-tester, or by hanging it from a semi-circular corona. For a canopy that is the height of

simplicity, you need nothing more than a large hook in the ceiling above the bed and a length of sheer fabric twisted and draped over it.

Your choice of fabric will help determine how dressed or undressed your bed – and hence your bedroom – appears. Heavy fabrics such as velvets and satins, especially lined with contrast material, will look rather formal, while sheers and lightweights have a more relaxed feel. Simple checked and striped cottons work well for a Scandinavian look and hessians and linens are a good choice for a natural, back-to-nature effect or for a masculine feel. A slightly period feel is not necessarily a prerequisite for drapes and hangings. If you use felt, men's suiting or tweeds, the result will be cutting-edge contemporary.

THIS PAGE This bed is dressed rather formally with a two-tone drape looped between narrow rods to form a canopy. The rest of the bed dressing is quite plain but the two-tone fabric is repeated in the footstool and over the headboard.

OPPOSITE LEFT An attractively carved wooden corona holds a graceful swathe of fabric which falls behind the bed as a headboard. The rest of the bed dressing is more understated though it looks supremely inviting.

OPPOSITE RIGHT This bed has drapes made from two simply tied old linen curtains. They are complemented by faded antique patchwork quilt whose colours echo the pale wood of the headboard.

THIS PAGE The finishing touches in this serene bedroom are provided by a pair of discreet wall lights, a potted orchid and a wooden box. There is no hint of excess to destroy the sense of calm.

Other Essentials

Although the bed is of prime importance in a bedroom, there are obviously a number of other essentials to take care of to the best of your ability when you are planning your decorative scheme. These essentials include the decoration of the walls, the kind of flooring you opt for, the type of window treatments you want, your choice of light fixtures and lamps, what form your bedroom storage will take and, not least, your choice of other furniture and of accessories such as lamps, mirrors and pictures. In addition, many of one's choices, especially when it comes to furniture, storage and light fittings, will be affected by exactly how multi-functional (or not) you intend to make your bedroom. Very feminine light fittings, for example, may not be practical enough to illuminate a work area in a bedroom-cum-office, just as a fragile Louis XV escritoire may not work as a serious desk.

Clearly, just as your choice of bed will have an effect on the style you are hoping to impart to your bedroom, so will your choice of these other elements. Hence they can, if carefully chosen, be used to underline that style and to chime with the tastes of the bedroom's users.

Finally, all one's choices do, of course, have to be within one's budget. One American designer I admire regards such costs as part of the 'investment' one is making. I tend to agree. At least I find it is more comforting to think of such expenses in that light.

TOP LEFT A long shallow window in a deliberately minimalist bedroom in a house in Australia is screened from the sun by effective metal venetian blinds. The floor is painted concrete.

TOP RIGHT White-stained and varnished floorboards give a clean, light look and are easy to maintain. For winter, you could make them look more cosy with a few rugs.

CENTRE LEFT A country-style cupboard with a limed finish stores an enormous amount of clothing but as it is light in colour, it does not overwhelm the smallish bedroom.

CENTRE RIGHT Lights that are at the correct height are essential for bedime reading, otherwise you risk a stiff neck and poor vision. Here an adjustable brushed-chrome light on a flexible arm is perfect for the job.

BOTTOM LEFT This two-tone dressing table with its deep drawer could be equally useful as a desk.

BOTTOM RIGHT A pretty display of delicate mirrors and pictures are grounded by the pair of dark lampshades above the bed.

WALLS

As is the case with most interior walls, those of the bedroom can either be plain- or faux-painted, papered, covered with fabric, wood, tile, polished plaster, polished concrete slabs, brick or even natural stone. Geographical location might help guide your choice, so if a particular material is indigenous to the place where you live, you will probably find that it looks good in your home.

Plain paint is generally the least expensive way to cover walls as long as they are in good condition. If they are not, you should remedy any problems so you can start with a smooth surface. This may mean filling in any cracks or larger holes, perhaps even re-plastering, and determining the cause of and eradicating any stains. Of course in an old country house you may well like the look of an uneven surface, but bear in mind that if you use a paint with a gloss or semi-gloss finish, any unevenness will be exaggerated.

BELOW LEFT A single wall of tongue-and-groove boards has been painted a taupe colour to form the perfect foil to the low white-dressed bed with its dark-wood frame.

BELOW Fabric-covered floor-to-ceiling panels behind this bed provide an unfussy background for the tailored headboard and inviting crisp white bedlinens and pillows.

THIS PAGE Large rectangular panels of blonde wood line an alcove that is the perfect size for the bed and its bedside tables and lamps. The choice of wood forms the basis for the mellow beige and spice-brown colour scheme.

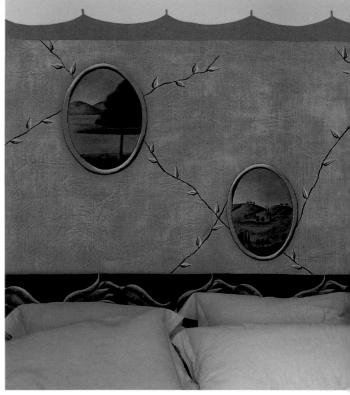

If your walls are seriously uneven, it may be best first to cover them with a heavy lining paper and then use a wallpaper of your choice on top. And what a choice of wallpaper there is, with colours and designs to suit all tastes and budgets. In addition to plains, stripes, graphic effects, large florals, small florals, mini-prints, over-scale prints and historic designs from the archives of the manufacturers, there are also wallpaper borders, wallpapers with textured effects, natural fibre papers, metallic papers and papers that imitate suede. There are also such realistic-looking faux-paint finish papers that you would be hard put to recognize the difference from real paint effects, and such papers can be far less expensive than calling in a professional painter.

FABRIC FINISH

Putting fabric on bedroom walls makes them look particularly luxurious, especially in a townhouse or apartment. The most cost-effective way to do this is to glue the fabric straight onto the wall yourself using special fabric glue, though unless you are both skilful and extremely patient, it is difficult to achieve a good result. Professional help will, of course, add to the cost. There are also clip systems on the market which you attach just above the skirting and below the ceiling. You then stretch lengths of fabric between the clips, taking the edges of the fabric really close up together. I find it advisable to paint the walls underneath the seams in exactly the same colour as the fabric so that any small

OPPOSITE LEFT In a Provençal cottage, toile de Jouy has been used not only for dressing the bed and for curtains, but has also been applied to the walls. The dark granite floor, wood trim and door make a pleasant contrast to all the flowers.

OPPOSITE RIGHT Fabric has again been used on a wall, but this time it is canvas painted with trompe l'œil landscapes in oval frames.

RIGHT This charming small guest bedroom features walls that have been painted in broad stripes of alternating white and beige. The stripes have even been continued over the shelf above the bed and are echoed in the narrower stripe of the bedspread. Despite the large scale of the stripes, the small room does not feel overwhelmed. The muted gold and pink colour scheme makes for a warm and inviting bedroom.

gaps will not be noticed. The best fabrics to use are close-woven fabrics – felts, flannels, suiting, heavy wools, firm, heavy cottons, hessians and cotton velvets.

Undoubtedly the softest and most sumptuous look of all is that provided by 'walling', which involves fixing battens to the walls, placing a thick polyester material known in the trade as 'bump' between the battens, and overlaying it all with seamed lengths of your chosen fabric. Joins are often covered with braid, particularly just under the ceiling and above the skirting boards.

OTHER WALL FINISHES

Stark minimalists in newly built or newly renovated buildings might like the look of polished plaster on their walls. Again, this is an effect that can best be produced by a professional. Or they might prefer the rugged, industrial look of concrete slabs, which again need to be professionally installed, especially as you must ensure the structure of your home is sufficiently strong. At the other extreme of the historical scale, if you strip the plaster from the walls of many period houses you often get down to some fine-looking, warm-coloured old bricks, which, once cleaned up and well-sealed to prevent crumbling and brick dust, will effect a great contrast with the soft surfaces of the bedroom, such as the bedding or curtains. You may be fortunate enough to have ancient-looking stone walls in your home. Though they may not be many people's

first choice for a bedroom, nevertheless they do look very dramatic.

Wood, whether as panelling, tongue-and-groove boards or rough-finished as in traditional log cabins, always looks warm and welcoming. Old panelling, which can be original to the home or can be bought from specialist salvage merchants, looks extremely distinguished and lends itself, of course, to distinguished antique beds and furniture. Panelling, like most wood, can either be left natural or can be stained or painted.

And finally, if you are something of an eco-warrior, you might like to try bamboo on your walls. Available in thin strips closely glued together and stained in various colours, these will bring the look of the Orient to your bedroom. What is more, you can sleep soundly in your bed in the knowledge that the bamboo on your walls has been sustainably harvested, and has grown in four or five years, far faster than slow-growing hardwoods.

ABOVE The walls of this new-build house in Suffolk, England are lined from floor to ceiling with beautifully figured wood that is a great foil to the crisp white bedding and oversized off-white padded headboard.

RIGHT This relatively new log cabin has been built with the pioneer aesthetic in mind and feels traditional and cosy. A print of an early settler and a quiver of arrows on the wall underscores that aesthetic, as does the Navajo throw on the bed.

OPPOSITE A historic house in Pennsylvania benefits from walls made from local fieldstone. In the bedroom, the owner has eschewed traditonal décor in favour of a low-slung contemporary bed and pieces of modern art.

FLOORS

On the whole, my preference is for bedroom floors to be soft and forgiving, or at least for there to be rugs by the bed. This is as much for comfort and warmth underfoot as for reducing noise. If the decision is for carpets, be sure to choose the right grade, usually described as 'bedroom grade'. This does not have the same hard-wearing quality or high price as carpet for rooms that have more foot traffic.

If you have stringent budgetary requirements and are refurbishing a bedroom, I do advise you not to make any radical decisions on floor coverings before studying the existing floors very carefully. You may well have solid wood floors – perhaps concealed by carpet – that are in reasonable condition or that can relatively easily be restored, and if softness underfoot is an issue, that can easily be addressed by using some rugs.

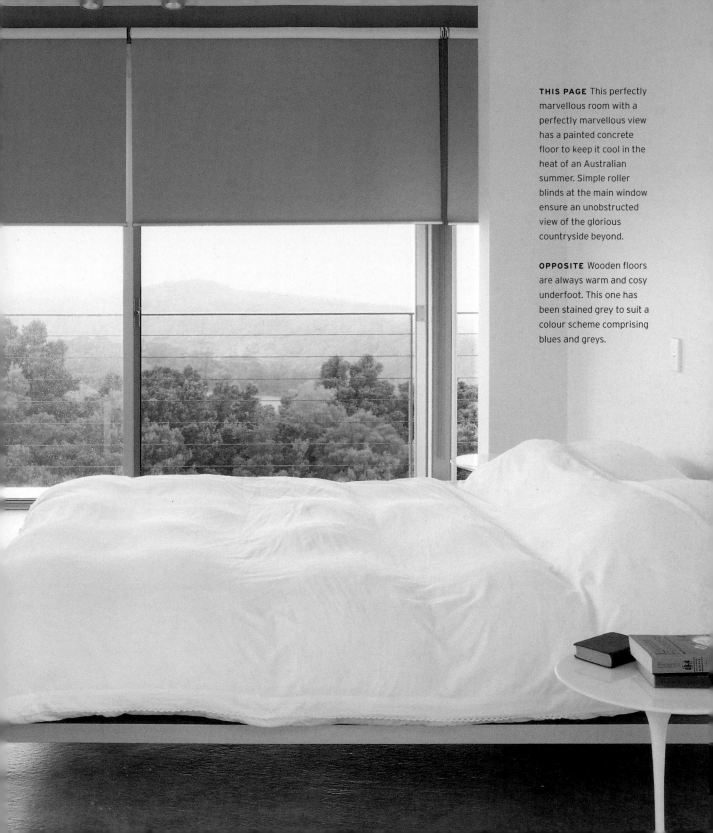

THIS PAGE This perfectly marvellous room with a perfectly marvellous view has a painted concrete floor to keep it cool in the heat of an Australian summer. Simple roller blinds at the main window ensure an unobstructed view of the glorious countryside beyond.

OPPOSITE Wooden floors are always warm and cosy underfoot. This one has been stained grey to suit a colour scheme comprising blues and greys.

THIS PAGE An all-white room with gloss-painted wooden floorboards is the epitome of cool minimalism. Perhaps surprisingly, it is in an eighteenth-century East London townhouse that has been stripped out inside to maximize the sense of light and space.

OPPOSITE A gleaming polished wood floor forms an unexpected contrast with the rough brickwork and semi-industrial feel of this loft apartment. Old Indian doors and tongue-and-groove panelling add a another two, totally different, wooden elements to the scene.

If you are lucky, perhaps your wooden floorboards will only need to be polished to restore them to their former glory. More drastic measures will require sanding and sealing, perhaps also staining, which allows the grain to show through, or painting.

If you like wooden floors but do not have one already, you can buy reclaimed floorboards or install a new wood floor. Certain woods such as mahogany and iroko are endangered, however, so buy only wood that has been certified by an internationally recognized organization such as the Forestry Stewardship Council (FSC), or perhaps consider a bamboo floor, which is very eco-friendly and has become rather chic of late.

If solid wood is beyond your means, a less expensive option is wood-laminate flooring. Easy to lay in sections that lock together or are simply glued to the subfloor, the best have a real wood veneer, while budget ranges have a simulated wood finish.

OTHER FLOORING MATERIALS

If you live in a hot climate, stone, such as marble, limestone and terrazzo — which is made of marble chips set in concrete — is enjoying great popularity and is very handsome, especially in a contemporary setting, but before installing a stone floor, you need to check that your floor joists can take the strain. Similar issues arise if you want a concrete floor. The look of this brutalist material can be softened by polishing or by the addition of a top layer of resin that can be coloured if you wish. The result is sleek, shiny and sophisticated and looks especially good in a loft apartment or a very modern building or renovation.

LEFT The pine floor in this stone-walled bedroom was reclaimed from an old barn. It forms the perfect backdrop to the contemporary furniture and stark white bed.

OPPOSITE ABOVE The high-gloss black wooden floorboards in this chic bedroom make the bed and chairs look as if they are floating on an island of white. The texture and colour of the rug contrast well with the shiny floor.

OPPOSITE BELOW In a Japanese-style bedroom, the mattress stands directly on tatami mats on rich wooden floorboards.

Other flooring choices include rubber, linoleum and even leather, all of which are soft, warm and resilient. Rubber comes in a huge range of colours and textures, while linoleum is making a comeback. Made from natural materials, it chimes well with today's environmental concerns. It comes in many colours, textures and patterns, and there are centrepieces, borders and made-to-order design options which are very handsome. Finally, leather – one of the most sumptuous and sensual of floorings, and with a price to match. Maintained properly – protect from bright sunlight and sharp heels, vacuum regularly and wax once or twice a year with natural beeswax – it will develop a lovely patina over time and last many years.

WINDOWS

One usually requires some sort of window treatment in a bedroom, if only for the sake of privacy. However, when it comes to deciding how to dress the windows, if you are a morning-light-lover and your bedroom partner is a morning-light-hater, this can be one of the biggest bones of decorating contention between you. It is a particularly contentious issue these days because many contemporary homeowners eschew the heavy lined, frilled and flounced curtain treatments of the 1980s, which were ideal for blocking the light, in favour of today's greatly pared-down look, which can be far from ideal for this purpose.

However, despite one's personal sleeping preferences, it is best to keep window coverings in keeping with the style of the rest of the room. Elaborately fringed and swagged curtains would look odd in a minimalist room, just as very brightly coloured blinds or curtains would not look right in a room with otherwise calm and gentle decoration.

As well as bearing in mind the context of your decorating scheme, you may have a beautiful window – or view – that you would not wish to hide. The most effective window-dressing solutions in this case, and also for a large picture window or wall of window that

THIS PAGE This off-white roman blind will gently filter the light but won't exclude it completely.

OPPOSITE TOP LEFT With two curtain poles at a bay window you can have voile curtains for privacy and for for filtering the light and heavier curtains to draw across at night. The heavier curtains hang from an angled pole that follows the contours of the bay.

OPPOSITE TOP RIGHT This Delhi bedroom has windows hung with semi-sheer tab-top curtains. One long pole holds two different panels of fabric to create an unusual decorative effect.

OPPOSITE BELOW LEFT A semi-sheer blue-and-white voile with blue edging hangs gracefully from a wooden pole in front of a deeply recessed window. The effect is fresh and feminine.

OPPOSITE BELOW RIGHT Multiple curtain tracks provide versatile screening. The sheerest curtain, next to the window, provides privacy in daytime. The other, heavier, curtains can be drawn across when privacy is required at night-time. Basket-topped cupboards either side of the window form a frame.

incorporates a sliding glass door, are always the simplest. Try unfussy roman or roller blinds, paper blinds, Swedish blinds, vertical blinds, venetian blinds with fine wood or metal fins, sheer panels or a system of sliding panels hung from ceiling tracks. For a softer look, you could always try a floor-length sheer curtain looped back on one side of the window, or just a lightweight valance attached to a batten above the window.

Bay windows can be tricky to deal with, but fortunately, if you want curtains, there are special bay-window curtain tracks on the market. Or, if you wish, you could combine a blind for each window of the bay with sham curtains looped back and attached to a hook on the wall either side.

French doors often open inwards which makes hanging curtains difficult. If possible, hang them from a pole that is longer than the door opening is wide, then they can be pulled well to the side to allow the doors to open. Alternatively, hang a blind against the glazed part of the door, or use a curtain on a portière rod. One end of this is fixed to the doorframe and when the door is opened, it hinges so the curtain can be swung back out of the way.

THIS PAGE Simple roller blinds are suspended neatly and invisibly between the ceiling and the glass in a beautifully situated bedroom that looks out over the woods beyond. The glazing continues beneath the floor of this room to the floor below.

OPPOSITE For a room with an unusual shape and a vast expanse of window, made up of almost seamlessly joined glass panels, a row of banner-like blinds provide versatile screening from strong sunlight. They also have a decorative effect.

LIGHTING

One of the main requirements in a bedroom is lighting for reading in bed, for which you will need lamps that project good light over the shoulder and onto the page. That can best be achieved with wall-mounted or floor-standing swing-arm light fixtures. You will also need ambient lighting (see pages 32–33). I can never understand why the lone central-light myth continues to be practised. A central pendant light can be used but, especially in a not-too-large bedroom, it is at least as effective and much more versatile and attractive to have a number of wall-mounted lights. Another alternative to the ubiquitous central light is to have small recessed downlights in the ceiling. These can be supplemented by some accent lighting to draw attention to, say, paintings or decorative objects.

Received wisdom dictates that a traditional decorative scheme demands traditional-style light fixtures, but if you have the confidence, it can instead be effective to use old fixtures or lamps in a modern room and elegant modern lights in a traditional room.

OPPOSITE LEFT A pretty chandelier trimmed with metal flowers underlines the delicate floral decoration of this pretty guest bedroom with its pair of beds.

OPPOSITE RIGHT In this all-white room, the industrial aesthetic created by the exposed stud timbers of the wall is perfectly echoed in the contemporary metal rise-and-fall light fixture hanging in one corner.

ABOVE A gleaming chrome adjustable reading light attached to the dark-wood headboard is both handsome and practical.

ABOVE RIGHT Swan-necked lamps perched high up on top of the oversized headboard emit a crisp white focused halogen light that is perfect for bedtime reading.

RIGHT A gold coloured Philippe Starck lamp casts an atmospheric light both up and down in this chic urban bedroom where it stands out as a dramatic focal point and object in its own right.

STORAGE

Whether your bedroom storage is to be a beautifully fitted out walk-in area, one that is custom-built, bought ready-made or somehow improvised, you will want to find pieces that enhance your decorative scheme. If you live in an old building and have a bedroom with a high ceiling and attractive mouldings that you would not want to conceal with floor-to-ceiling built-in cupboards, at least some of your storage needs might be catered for with a freestanding armoire or old wardrobe. Large old pieces can often be bought gratifyingly cheaply since they are generally too tall and wide for contemporary rooms, and the interior can often be reconfigured to hold an extraordinary quantity of clothes, shoes, underwear, sweaters and shirts. For example, you may well be able to lower a

clothes rail in such a piece of furniture in order to leave space for a shelf on top, or you could have two tiers of clothes rails to cater for shorter and longer clothes.

Retro furniture and reclaimed fixtures and fittings offer other freestanding storage possibilities. Many stylish contemporary bedrooms have been based on pieces such as old plan chests and shop fitments, or on fifties and sixties chests of drawers or shelf units.

BUILT-IN FURNITURE CHOICES

You can have built-in furniture custom-made for you, you can go to a specialist bedroom fitment supplier, or you can buy ready-made and install it yourself. Ready-made storage furniture comes in a huge variety of styles and finishes to choose from that will suit both

FAR LEFT A neat retro-style shelf unit provides a storage space above a bed.

LEFT The sloping walls of this attic bedroom preclude much hanging space, but they provide the perfect spot to locate a chest of drawers.

OPPOSITE This super-tall headboard is flanked by floor-to-ceiling storage consisting of shelves, cupboards and drawers, and also a pair of bedside tables. The whole has been lacquered to match the room's decorative scheme.

THIS PAGE This bedroom possesses the ultimate luxury – a walk-in dressing room with fitted storage. This bank of drawers, rather like a plan chest, will house a great deal of clothing and looks beautiful, as well.

OPPOSITE In the case of this elegant dressing room, an enormous amount of hanging space is concealed behind chocolate-brown velvet curtains.

traditional and contemporary decorating schemes, and in materials ranging from wood and medium-density fibreboard (MDF) to glass and metal.

If having it custom-made, you may wish to consider making your built-in furniture seem part of the walls by using the same decorative treatment on both, whether that is paint, wallpaper or a fabric covering. Paint and wallpaper finishes can be given a coat or two of matt or eggshell polyurethane varnish which will make them much tougher. Another alternative is to have louvered wardrobe doors, or mirrored doors, which will make the bedroom look much larger.

And one final tip: when installing built-in-furniture, try to ensure that the cupboards reach ceiling height, by adding top cupboards if necessary. Few things spoil the proportions of a room as much as an unsightly gap between the top of a wardrobe and a ceiling, quite apart from the fact that it is a waste of space and a dust trap. If the top cupboards are then very high, you can put your least-used objects up there and reach them when necessary with a pair of steps.

OTHER FURNITURE

Although the bed is clearly the most important piece of furniture in any bedroom and often sets the style, that style is certainly rounded out by the other furniture in the room. Comfortable chairs, occasional chairs, stools, chaises longues, daybeds, small sofas, bedside and other side tables, including dressing tables – which are not often seen today as most women put on their make-up in the bathroom – and desks, all add character to the room even if there is only space for very few extra pieces. All such occasional furniture comes in a wide range of styles and finishes and at prices to suit every budget.

As a designer who is concerned with comfort, I do not like to see a bed without a pair of bedside tables or small chests of drawers beside it. At the very least, I like there to be an occasional chair alongside the bed that can be used as a place to put one's bedtime reading. This will suffice as long as there is a wall light or lights on the wall behind the bed. In fact, I would certainly always want to see at least one chair in the bedroom and, as long as there is space, a piece of occasional furniture at the end of the bed, such as an upholstered stool, a chaise longue or a small sofa.

DOUBLE-DUTY FURNITURE

If space is at a premium, you may have to make your occasional furniture work twice as hard. Instead of an upholstered stool at the foot of the bed, have a low

LEFT A large, comfortable wing chair looks good in a room whose ceiling beams have been painted to match the chair's upholstery. The graphic red-and-white patchwork quilt stands in stark contrast to the room's gentle faded florals.

OPPOSITE TOP LEFT A beamed attic room has space for a small deep-buttoned couch as well as for a pair of bedside tables, a chest of drawers and an occasional chair. The disparate elements of furniture are united by the neutral floor matting.

OPPOSITE TOP RIGHT An early nineteenth-century bed is partnered with an eclectic choice of furniture – an unusual round table, a leather-covered chair and a chest of drawers.

OPPOSITE BELOW LEFT The owner of this very personal bedroom has also included a slightly down-at-heel but still elegant buttoned daybed.

OPPOSITE BELOW RIGHT In a seaside bedroom, a wicker chair adds a holiday feel. Wicker is very light to move so makes ideal bedroom chairs.

chest which can be used for storing spare bedding; do not have a dressing table, but a table that can be both make-up area and occasional desk; rather than a chaise longue, consider an armchair with matching padded footstool whose lid lifts to reveal some storage space.

Since the ancillary furniture in the bedroom is usually less costly than the bed and mattress, storage furniture and window and floor treatments, it is quite possible to change the look of the room completely from time to time either by exchanging one or two pieces of furniture for pieces in a different style, or by painting the furniture. In the same vein, you could re-cover an upholstered chair, sofa or headboard to coordinate with new bedding.

ABOVE With scant space for a bedside table, this one – scarcely more than a drawer on a curved leg – is perfect. The wall-mounted light saves space on the surface of the table.

OPPOSITE A pale wood shelf-like bedside table, a pair of low stone and metal tables and a sinuous wooden chair help to enhance the strongly linear, Japanese-inspired theme of this bedroom with its shoji screen walls. Dramatic plants complete the picture.

RIGHT This discreet bedside table with an unusual woven shelf also serves as the starting point for a considered display of accessories.

ACCESSORIES

People are always saying, quite rightly, that accessories in a room are like jewellery on a woman. They are meant to enhance the room, just as jewellery enhances a woman's looks and clothes.

Generally speaking, just as you do not put on your jewellery until you have finished dressing, so you do not start thinking about the accessories until the rest of the bedroom has been finished to your satisfaction. On occasion, though, there are one or two accessories that you already own and treasure that have actually formed the basis of your decorative scheme: a painting, for example, a set of prints, a rug, a mirror, a collection of old glass or a piece of sculpture.

If this is not the case, you will almost certainly go shopping for accessories. Nowadays, of course, the shops are full of attractive decorative objects to suit all bedroom styles, and it is certainly possible to buy new every few years to update your bedroom look. However, especially since the bedroom is the one room in the house where there is no need to please anyone but yourself, I recommend that you try to include items that are really personal to you, even if they are nothing more than a collection of photographs of family and friends, some favourite posters, a few found objects from a family holiday, or even some framed pieces of fabric that you particularly like.

THIS PAGE A gilt dressing-table mirror complements perfectly the feminine, romantic feel of this charming bedroom.

OPPOSITE FAR LEFT An eclectic collection of an old painted wood column, an urn, some pictures and a small statue form their own composition.

OPPOSITE LEFT A collection of prints and mirrors and a pretty vase of flowers add character to this bedroom.

- If you are arranging a 'still life' on a bedside table, be sure to leave some space for books and other bedside necessities.

- The unexpected often has greater impact than the expensive.

- Do not forget the value of a plant or beautiful vase of fragrant flowers in bringing life to a bedroom display.

- Try out arrangements of pictures on the floor first.

- Avoid the temptation of having too many 'star' pieces as they tire the eye.

OPPOSITE Muted green picture frames and white mounts unite this collection of twelve French prints, as does hanging them in one large, well-balanced block. They fill the wall space perfectly and help to balance the bulk of the fireplace with its mirror above, both of which are painted in the same green.

RIGHT The objects on this side table have been chosen for the way their colours enhance the rich shades of camel and coffee in the room. The beautiful orchid adds a soft touch as well as height to the display.

Arranging Accessories

If furniture is what makes a room habitable and comfortable, then accessories are what gives it personality. Because people's memorabilia are generally rather diverse, their arrangement should involve a thoughtful assembly of texture, shape and colour, just as a painter or a photographer arranges a still life. Group rather than scatter small objects, for example display one or two family photographs on a bedside table or windowsill, assemble shells or polished stones in goblets, or group a number of photographs in a single, unifying frame. Similarly with a collection of prints – give them a sense of unity by mounting them on the same colour and using matching frames. When grouping larger objects, look for a unifying theme such as colour or texture, or simply use a single beautiful object on its own as a focal point, giving added impact at night with a spotlight above or below.

Suppliers

UK BED SUPPLIERS

AND SO TO BED
(contemporary and traditional designs)
Tel: + 44 (0) 808 144 4343
www.andsotobed.com

NATURAL BED COMPANY
(as the name implies)
168-170 Devonshire Street
Sheffield S3 7SG
Tel: + 44 (0) 114 272 1984

ORIGINAL BEDSTEAD
(handcrafted classic and old styles)
Tel: + 44 (0) 1536 407 138
www.obc-uk.net

SAVOIR BEDS
(any bed made to order)
Tel: + 44 (0) 20 7486 2222

SILENTNIGHT BEDS
(large range of beds, including beds with drawers beneath; also padded headboards)
PO Box 9
Barnoldswick,
Lancs BB18 6BL
Tel: + 44 (0) 1282 851 111

SIMON HORN
(particularly for traditional French styles)
117-121 Wandsworth Bridge Road
London SW6 2TP
Tel: + 44 (0) 207 736 1754

SIMON TAYLOR
(individually designed beds and headboards)
Cane End Lane
Bierton
Aylesbury
Bucks HP22 5BH
Tel: + 44 (0) 1296 488 207

THE LONDON WALLBED COMPANY
(good wall and Murphy beds, wardrobes, etc.)
430 Chiswick High Road
London W4 5TF
Tel: + 44 (0) 20 8742 8200

THE WALLBED WORKSHOP
290 Battersea Park Road
London SW11 3BT
Tel: + 44 (0) 20 7924 5300
www.thewallbedworkshop.co.uk

USA AND INTERNATIONAL BED SUPPLIERS

ABC CARPET & HOME
(excellent selection of all styles)
881/888 Broadway
New York NY 1003
Tel: +1 (212) 473 3000
or to find a store near you:
+1 800 GO BEYOND
www.abchomes.com

A BRASS BED SHOPPE
(brass and iron beds)
13800 Miles Avenue
Cleveland
Ohio 44105
Tel: + 1 (216) 371 0400
www.brassbedshoppe.com

B & B ITALIA
(elegant contemporary Italian beds; stores worldwide)
www.bebitalia.it/bebitalia-home

BAKER FURNITURE
(splendid classic styles; stores across US)
www.baker.kohlerinteriors.com

CALVIN KLEIN HOME
(great beds in general; branches worldwide)
Phillips-Van Heusen Corporation
200 Madison Avenue
New York NY 10016

CALLIGARIS ITALIAN LIVING
(sophisticated contemporary Italian designs)
www.calligaris.it

CHARLES P. ROGERS
(huge choice of classic, sleigh, canopy beds, daybeds, trundle beds, leather and contemporary beds, plus interesting headboards; stores in New York and New Jersey)
Manhattan Tel: + 1 (212) 675 4400
New Jersey Tel: + 1 (201) 933 8300

DOMUS DESIGN COLLECTION
(distinctive contemporary and box-storage beds)
181 Madison Avenue
New York NY 10016
Tel: + 1 (212) 685 0800

GRANGE
(handmade French cherrywood beds in a range of hand-applied colour finishes; stockists worldwide)

HOB NAIL ANTIQUES INC
(great selection of antique brass and iron beds)
1151 Route 22
Pawling NY 12564
Tel: + 1 (845) 855 1623

UK MATTRESSES

ALPHABEDS
(nine different sorts of mattress, any size)
92 Tottenham Court Road
London W1T 4TL
Tel: + 44 (0) 20 7636 6840

AND SO TO BED
(mattresses and bedheads as well as beds and bedding)

BEDS LTD
(Supplier of big brand mattresses: Silentnight: Sealy; Layezee etc.)
220 North End Road
London W14 9NX
Tel: + 44 (0) 20 7385 7711

CITYBEDS
(budget to luxury mattresses from Sealy, Silentnight; Healthbeds, Hypnos, Myers and Staples)
17 Gibbins Road
Stratford
London E15 2HU
Tel: + 44 (0) 20 8534 9000

LITVINOFF & FAWCETT (natural filled and top-quality spring, handmade bespoke mattresses at mass-produced prices)
281 Hackney Road
London E2 8NA
Tel: + 44 (0) 20 7739 3840

SILENTNIGHT BEDS
(spring and foam mattresses)
PO Box 9
Barnoldswick
Lancs BB18 6BL
Tel: + 44 (0) 1282 851 111

USA AND INTERNATIONAL MATTRESSES

HASTENS
(Swedish company offering 'the world's most exclusive beds'; stores worldwide)

SEALY
(pressure-relieving mattresses, spring mattresses; also beds and headboards; products available worldwide)
One Office Parkway at
Sealy Drive
Trinity
NC 27370
Tel + 1 (336) 861 3500
www.sealyinc.com

TEMPUR
(pressure-relieving, Swedish mattresses and pillows)

VI-SPRING
(mattresses as well as complete beds and headboards; European stockists)
Ernesettle Lane
Ernesettle
Plymouth PL5 2TT
Tel: + 44 (0) 1752 366 311
www.vispring.co.uk

UK BEDLINENS AND BEDDING

The following companies are useful sources as are the linen departments of good department stores.

AND SO TO BED
(fine linens, throws, etc., as well as beds; locations throughout the UK)
Tel: + 44 (0) 808 144 4343

ANTIQUE DESIGNS LTD
(exquisite replicas of antique bedlinen)
Ash House
Ash Lane
Little Leigh
Northwich
Cheshire CW8 4RG
Tel: + 44 (0) 1606 892 822/3

ARMOIRE LINEN COMPANY
(fine linens in exceptional Egyptian cotton)
Beech House
Beech Farm Drive
Macclesfield SK10 2ER
Tel: + 44 (0) 1625 431 166

BEYOND FRANCE (handspun vintage linens from Hungary)
Tel: + 44 (0) 7710 148 915

CABBAGES & ROSES
(pretty, old-fashioned designs)
3 Langton Street
London SW10 0JL
Tel: + 44 (0) 20 7252 7333

FOREVER ENGLAND
(delectable linens and quilts; shops in Sherborne, Dorset and Lymington, Hants)
Tel: + 44 (0) 870 241 6517
(mail-order enquiries)
www.foreverengland.net

JOSEPHINE HOME (beautiful bedlinen and cashmere throws)
Chelsea Harbour
Design Centre
3rd Floor
South Dome
London SW10 0XE
Tel: + 44 (0) 800 0778278

KING OF COTTON
(fine linens at wholesale prices)
Unit 5 Sandycombe Centre
1-9 Sandycombe Road
Richmond-on-Thames
Surrey TW9 2EP
Tel: + 44 (0) 20 8332 7999

MARGARET MUIR
(beautiful embroidered linens and bedding)
Tel: + 44 (0) 845 450 5667

MONOGRAMMED LINEN SHOP
(sumptuous bedlinens, etc.)
168-170 Walton Street
London SW3 2JL
Tel: + 44 (0) 20 7589 4033

THE ORIGINAL ENGLISH CUSTOM COVER
(made-to-measure bedlinen for awkwardly shaped beds)
Holmfirth
West Yorks HD9 3XR
Tel: + 44 (0) 845 226 7388

USA AND INTERNATIONAL BEDLINEN AND BEDDING

All good department stores including branches of Crate & Barrel
(www.crateandbarrel.com)
Bed, Bath & Beyond
(www.bedbathandbeyond.com)
and Pottery Barn
(www.potterybarn.com) for good inexpensive selections.

ANTIQUE QUILT SOURCE
(American quilts, 1850–1940)
Dept. www
3064 Bricker Road
Manheim PA 17545–9644
Tel: + 1 (717) 492 9876

BEST DRESSED BED COLLECTION
(my own range of co-ordinating duvets, bedskirts, pillows, cushions, table skirts, bed and window curtains in 5 styles)
Décor & You
900 Main Street,
Building #2
Southbury
Connecticut 06488
Tel: + 1 (203) 264 3500
www.decorandyou.com

HOUSEHOLD LINENS
(beautiful and original bedding
and bedlinens with stores in
Australia and New Zealand;
worldwide shipping)
Mail Order
PO Box 37046
Parnell
Auckland
New Zealand
Tel: + 64 (0) 9 366 0712
www.household-linens.com

ROSE & HEATHER
(idiosyncratic and interesting
bedding and linens with stores
in Australia and New Zealand;
worldwide shipping)
P.O. Box 46-014
Herne Bay
Auckland 1
New Zealand
Tel: + 64 (0) 9 520 4442
www.roseandheather.co.nz

Architects & Designers

1100 ARCHITECT
435 Hudson Street
New York NY 10014
USA
Tel: +1 (212) 645 1011
www.1100architect.com

ABRAHAM & THAKORE LTD
D351 Defence Colony
New Delhi 110024
India
Tel: + 91 11 699 3714

ALEX VAN DE WALLE
Vlaamsesteenweg 3
1000 Brussels
Belgium
Tel: + 32 (0)477 806 676
alex.vdw@swing.be

ANDERSON MASON DALE
ARCHITECTS
1615 Seventeenth Street
Denver Colorado 80202
USA
Tel: +1 (303) 294 9448
www.amdarchitects.com

ANDRÉE PUTMAN SARL
83 avenue Denfert-Rochereau
75014 Paris
France
Tel: + 33 (0) 1 55 42 88 55
www.andreeputman.com

ATELIER D'ARCHITECTURE M
FRISENNA SCPL
15 rue de Verviers
4020 Liège
Belgium
Tel: + 32 (0) 4 341 5786

BALDASSARE LA RIZZA
London House
Suite 13a
266 Fulham Road
London SW10 9EL
Tel: + 44 (0) 20 7351 5771
www.larizza.com

BILHUBER & ASSOCIATES
330 East 59th Street
New York NY 10022
USA
Tel: + 1 (212) 308 4888
www.bilhuber.com

BRAY-SCHAIBLE DESIGN INC
80 West 40th Street
New York
NY 10018
Tel: +1 (212) 354 7525

CATHERINE MEMMI
11 rue Saint Sulpice
75006 Paris
France
Tel: + 33 (0) 1 44 07 22 28
Tel: + 1 (212) 226 8200
www.catherinememmi.com

CHRISTOPHE GOLLUT
116 Fulham Road
London SW3 6HU
Tel: + 44 (0) 20 7370 4021
www.christophegollut.com

CLINTON MURRAY
ARCHITECTS
2 King Street
Merimbula
New South Wales 2548
Australia
Tel: + 61 (0) 2 6495 1964
www.clintonmurray.com.au

COLLECTION PRIVÉE
9 rue des États-Unis
06400 Cannes
France
Tel: + 33 (0) 4 97 06 94 94
www.collection-privee.com

COLLETT-ZARZYCKI
Fernhead Studios
2b Fernhead Road
London W9 3ET
Tel: + 44 (0) 20 8969 6967
www.collett-zarzycki.com

COORENGEL & CALVAGRAC
43 rue de l'Echiquier
75010 Paris
France
Tel: + 33 (0) 1 40 27 14 65
www.coorengel-calvagrac.com

DOMINIQUE KIEFFER
8 rue Hérold
75001 Paris
France
Tel: + 33 (0) 1 42 21 32 44
www.dkieffer.com

DRAKE DESIGN ASSOCIATES
315 East 62nd Street
NY NY 10021
USA
Tel: + 1 (212) 754 3099
www.drakedesignassociates.com

ENGELEN MOORE
44 McLachlan Avenue
Rushcutters Bay
Sydney
New South Wales 2011
Australia
Tel: + 61 2 9380 4099
www.ianmoorearchitects.com

ÉRIC GIZARD ASSOCIÉS
14 rue Crespin du Cast
75011 Paris
France
Tel: + 33 (0)1 55 28 38 58
www.gizardassocies.com

FORMA DESIGNS
Luigi Esposito
160 Walton Street
London SW3 2JL
Tel: + 44 (0) 20 7581 2500
www.formadesigns.co.uk

FRANK FAULKNER
92 North 5th Street
Hudson
New York NY 12534
USA
Tel: + 1 (518) 828 2295

FRED COLLIN
Bransdale Lodge
Bransdale Fadmor
York YO62 7JL
Tel: + 44 (0)1751 431 137
fred@fscollin.demon.co.uk

HEIBERG CUMMINGS DESIGN
9 West 19th Street
3rd Floor
New York NY 10011
USA
Tel: + 1 (212) 337 2030
www.hcd3.com

HENNIE INTERIORS AS
Helene Forbes-Hennie
Thomles Gate 4
0270 Oslo
Norway
Tel: + 47 22 06 85 86

HOLLY LUEDERS
36 East 72nd Street
New York NY 10021
USA
Tel: + 1 (212) 535 6651

INDIGO SEAS
123 Nth Robertson Boulevard
Los Angeles
California 90048-3101
Tel: + 1 (310) 550 8758

JAMES MOHN DESIGN
245 West 29th Street
Suite 504
New York NY 10001
USA
Tel: + 1 (212) 414 1477
www.jamesmohndesign.com

JOHN BARMAN INC
500 Park Avenue
Suite 12a
New York NY 10022
USA
Tel: + 1 (212) 838 9443
www.johnbarman.com

JULIE PRISCA
46 rue du Bac
75007 Paris
France
Tel: + 33 (0) 1 45 48 13 29
www.julieprisca.com

KATHARINE POOLEY
160 Walton Street
London SW3 2JL
Tel: + 44 (0) 20 7584 3223
www.katharinepooley.com

KATHRYN M IRELAND
1619 Stanford Street
Santa Monica
California 90404
USA
Tel: + 1 (310) 315 4351
www.kathrynireland.com

KELLY HOPPEN
2 Munden Street
London W14 0RH
Tel: + 44 (0) 20 7471 3350
www.kellyhoppen.com

KENYON KRAMER
Décoration Jardin
3 place des 3 Ormeaux
13100 Aix en Provence
France
Tel: + 33 (0) 4 42 23 52 32

LARRY LASLO
240 East 67th Street
Suite A
New York NY 10021
USA
Tel: + 1 (212) 734 3824
www.larrylaslodesigns.com

LAURENCE KRIEGEL
Loladesign2002@yahoo.com

LENA PROUDLOCK
4 The Chipping
Tetbury
Gloucestershire GL8 8ET
Tel: + 44 (0)1666 500 051
www.lenaproudlock.com

LEONARDO CHALUPOWICZ
3527 Landa Street
Los Angeles
California 90039
USA
Tel: + 1 (323) 660 8261
www.chalupowicz.com

LINUM FRANCE SAS
ZAC du Tourail
Coustellet
84660 Maubec
France
Tel: + 33 (0) 4 90 76 34 00
www.linum-france.com

MARTIN BRUDNIZKI DESIGN
STUDIO
Unit 2L
Chelsea Reach
79-89 Lots Road
London SW10 0RN
Tel: + 44 (0) 20 7376 7555
www.mbds.net

MICHAEL TRAPP
7 River Road
Box 67 West Cornwall
Connecticut 06796
USA
Tel: + 1 (860) 672 6098

MICHAEL WOLFSON
ARCHITECTS
(London, England)
Tel: + 44 (0) 20 7630 9377

MURIEL BRANDOLINI
525 East 72nd Street
New York NY 10021
USA
Tel: + 1 (212) 249 4920
www.murielbrandolini.com

NATHALIE HAMBRO
63 Warwick Square
London SW1V 2AL
Tel: + 44 (0) 20 7834 1122
www.fullofchic.com

NATHALIE LÉTÉ
Tel: + 33 (0) 1 49 60 84 76
www.nathalie-lete.com

NICOLAS VIGNOT
6, rue Vaucouleurs
75011 PARIS
Tel: + 33 (0) 6 11 96 67 69
http://n.vignot.free.fr

OLIVIER GAGNÈRE &
ASSOCIÉS
47 boulevard Saint-Jacques
75014 Paris
France
Tel: + 33 (0) 1 45 80 79 67

PIERRE D'AVOINE ARCHITECTS
54-58 Tanner Street
London SE1 3PH
Tel: + 44 (0) 20 7403 7220
www.davoine.net

RAMÓN ESTEVE
Estudio de Arquitectura
Jorge Juan 8, 5°, 11a
46004 Valencia
Spain
Tel: + 34 96 351 0434
www.ramonesteve.com

REED DESIGN
151a Sydney Street
London SW3 6NT
Tel: + 44 (0) 20 7565 0066

RESISTANCE DESIGN
Eric Mailaender
11 Tompkins Place, no.2
Brooklyn
NY 11231
Tel: +1 (212) 714 0448
www.resistancedesign.com

SALLY SIRKIN LEWIS
J ROBERT SCOTT
8737 Melrose Avenue
Los Angeles
California 90069
USA
Tel: + 1 (310) 659 4910
www.jrobertscott.com

SELLDORF ARCHITECTS
62 White Street
New York NY 10013
USA
Tel: + 1 (212) 219 9571
www.selldorf.com

SERA HERSHAM LOFTUS
Sera of London
3 Lonsdale Road
Notting Hill Gate
London W11 2BY
Tel: + 44 (0) 20 7467 0799
www.seraoflondon.com

SETH STEIN ARCHITECTS
15 Grand Union Centre
West Row
London W10 5AS
Tel: + 44 (0) 20 8968 8581
www.sethstein.com

SHARLAND & LEWIS
52 Long Street
Tetbury
Gloucestershire GL8 8AQ
Tel: + 44 (0) 1666 500354
www.sharlandandlewis.com

SLEE ARCHITECTS &
INTERIORS
101 Dorp Street
Stellenbosch 7600
South Africa
Tel: + 27 21 887 3385
www.slee.co.za

SOLIS BETANCOURT
1739 Connecticut Avenue NW
Washington
DC 20009
USA
Tel: + 1 (202) 659 8734
www.solisbetancourt.com

STEPHEN FALCKE INTERIOR
DESIGN CONSULTANTS
P O Box 1416
Parklands
Johannesburg 2121
South Africa
Tel: + 27 113 27 67 30

STICKLAND COOMBE
ARCHITECTS
258 Lavender Hill
London SW11 1LJ
Tel: + 44 (0) 20 7924 1699

STUDIO K O
Karl Fournier & Olivier Marty
7, Rue Geoffroy l'Angevin
75004 Paris
France
Tel: + 33 (0) 1 42 71 13 92
komarrakech@studioko.fr
koparis@studioko.fr

TED RUSSELL
Tel: + 1 (310) 275 1609

TERRY HUNZIKER INC
208 3rd Avenue South
Seattle
Washington 98104
USA
Tel: + 1 (206) 467 1144

THAD HAYES DESIGN INC
80 West 40th Street
New York NY 10018
USA
Tel: + 1 (212) 571 1234
www.thadhayes.com

TODHUNTER EARLE
Chelsea Reach
79-89 Lots Road
London SW10 0RN
Tel: + 44 (0) 20 7349 9999
www.todhunterearle.com

TRISTAN AUER
5a cour de la Métaine
75020 Paris
France
Tel: + 33 (0) 1 43 49 57 20

USHIDA FINDLAY (UK) LTD
1 Fitzroy Street
London W1T 4BQ
Tel: + 44 (0) 20 7755 2917
www.ushida-findlay.com

VINCENT VAN DUYSEN
Lombardenvest 34
2000 Antwerp
Belgium
Tel: + 32 (0) 3 205 9190
www.vanduysen.be

VICENTE WOLF ASSOCIATES
333 West 39th Street
New York NY 10019
USA
Tel: + 1 (212) 465 0590
www.vicentewolfassociates.com

VOORSANGER & ASSOCIATES
246 West 38th Street
New York NY 10018
USA
Tel: + 1 (212) 302 6464
www.voorsanger.com

Acknowledgements

PHOTOGRAPHERS' CREDITS

Ken Hayden 4, 12-13, 24 right, 30-31, 37 above, 54 left, 54-55, 63 left, 70-71, 82, 88-89, 102-103, 105 below left, 126-127, & 131.

Vincent Knapp 32 & 117 above.

David Ross 28

Simon Upton 1, 3 right, 9, 11 left, 15 centre left & right, 16, 17 below left, 18, 22, 25 above, 26 below, 27, 33, 38-39, 42, 44-45, 47 above right, 48, 50, 58-59, 60-61, 65, 66, 67 below, 68, 69 left, 72 right, 79 above right and centre, 80 below right, 83 below, 84, 86, 87 left, 92 above left, 94, 97, 98 right, 99 left, 101, 105 above right & centre, 108 left, 110 below, 111, 112, 114-116, 119 left, 122 left, 124 right, 129 above left & below right & 144.

Frederic Vasseur 10 left, 15 above right, 23, 24 left, 29 left, 63 right, 67 above, 76-77, 79 below left, 81, 92 above right, 100 left, 105 below right, 110 above, 118, 122 right, 132 right & 133.

Luke White endpapers, 5, 7, 17 above left, 19, 25 below, 28, 40, 47 centre left & below, 51 below, 52, 55 above & below, 69 right, 73, 80 left, 83 above, 91, 93, 95, 119 below right, 123 below, 125 & 134-135.

Andrew Wood front cover, 2, 3 left, 8, 10 right, 11 right, 15 above left & below, 17 above right, 17 below right, 20-21, 22 left, 26 above, 29 right, 34-35, 36, 37 below, 47 above left & centre right, 49, 51 above, 53, 56-57, 62, 64, 72 left, 74-75, 79 above left & below right, 80 above right, 87 right, 90, 92 below, 96, 98 left, 99 right , 100 right, 105 above left, 106-107, 108 right, 109, 112-113, 117 below, 119 above right, 120-121, 123 above, 124 left, 128, 129 above right & below left, 130 & 132 left.

SUPPLIERS CREDITS

85 left picture courtesy of Sealy; 85 right luxury pocket sprung mattress from And So To Bed

LOCATION CREDITS

Endpapers a riverside apartment in London, designed by Luigi Esposito; 1 a home featuring Jane Churchill fabrics; 2 Graham Head (of ABC Carpet & Home) and Barbara Rathborne's house in Long Island; 3 left a house in Connecticut designed by Michael Trapp; 3 right a home featuring Jane Churchill fabrics; 4 designed by Jackie Villevoye; 5 Kenneth Wyse's house in East Hampton designed by Larry Laslo for LL Designs; 7 a riverside apartment in London, designed by Luigi Esposito; 8 an apartment in Brussels designed by Vincent van Duysen; 9 a house in Virginia designed by Solis Betancourt; 10 left Reed & Delphine Krakoff's Manhattan townhouse, designed by Delphine Krakoff of Pamplemousse Design Inc.; 10 right Christophe Gollut's house in Gran Canaria; 11 left a home featuring Jane Churchill fabrics; 11 right Designer, Nathalie Hambro's apartment in London; 12-13 Patrick de Poortere's apartment, designed by Andrée Putman; 15 above left Christophe Gollut's house in Gran Canaria; 15 above right James Falla & Lynn Graham's house in Guernsey, designed by James Falla at MOOArc; 15 centre left a home featuring Jane Churchill fabrics; 15 centre right a farmhouse near Toulouse designed by Kathryn Ireland; 15 below left a house in Marrakech, designed by Karl Fournier and Olivier Marty, Studio KO; 15 below right Tristan Auer's apartment in Paris; 16 a home featuring Jane Churchill fabrics; 17 above left Catherine Memmi's house in Normandy; 17 above right design by Jasper Conran; 17 below left a home featuring Jane Churchill fabrics; 17 below right a house in Marrakech, designed by Karl Fournier and Olivier Marty, Studio KO; 18 a mountain retreat in Colorado, designed by Ron Mason; 19 Jamie Drake's East Hampton Home; 20 a house in Balnarring in coastal Victoria, designed by John Wardle Architects; 21 a house in Tuscon, Arizona, garden designed by Steve Martino, interior design by Voorsanger & Associates; 22 left Paolo Badesco's villa in Italy; 22 above right Yvonne Sporre's house in London, designed by J F Delsalle; 22 below right a home featuring Jane Churchill fabrics; 23 Nicolas Vignot's apartment in Paris, designed by Nicolas Vignot; 24 left James Falla & Lynn Graham's house in Guernsey, designed by James Falla at MOOArc; 24 right designed by Martin Brudnizki; 25 above left a mountain retreat in Colorado, designed by Ron Mason; 25 above right Tigmi, Morocco, designed by Max Lawrence; 25 below Catherine Memmi's house in Normandy; 26 above a house near Grasse, France, designed by Collett-Zarzycki Architects & Designers; 26 below a house in Virginia designed by Solis Betancourt; 27 Michael Leva's house in Connecticut; 28 a house in South Africa, designed by Stephen Falcke; 29 left Nina Gustafsson's Swedish home; 29 right a house in Ibiza, designed by Ramón Esteve Architects; 30-31 designed by Robert Bray & Mitchell Turnbough of Bray-Schaible Design Inc.; 32 interior design by Kelly Hoppen; 33 a house in New York designed by Stephen Roberts; 34 left a house near Cape Town designed by Johann Slee; 34 right a house in Italy designed by Paolo Badesco; 35 a house in New South Wales designed by Clinton Murray; 36 Mr & Mrs Boucquiau's house in Belgium, designed by Marina Frisenna; 37 above an interior designed by Sally Sirkin Lewis; 37 below Weaving/Thomasson residence, Essex; 38 Mrs Fasting's cabin in the Norwegian mountains, interior design by Heiberg Cummings Design; 39 Mr & Mrs Stokke's cabin in the Norwegian mountains, interior design by Helene Forbes-Hennie; 40 a riverside apartment in London, designed by Luigi Esposito; 42 Architect Gilles Pellerin's house in Cannes; 44-45 a home featuring Jane Churchill fabrics; 47 above left a house in Connecticut designed by Michael Trapp; 47 above right Alex van de Walle's apartment in Brussels; 47 centre left James Gager and Richard Ferretti's New York apartment designed in conjunction with Stephen Roberts; 47 centre right a house in Delhi, designed by Abraham & Thakore; 47 below left a riverside apartment in London, designed by Luigi Esposito; 47 below right Bernie de le Cuona's Windsor house; 48 designed by Stickland Coombe Architecture; 49 Richard & Lucille Lewin's House In Plettenberg Bay South Africa, designed by Seth Stein; 50 a home featuring Jane Churchill fabrics; 51 above a house in Connecticut designed by Michael Trapp; 51 below the Soho Hotel, London designed by Kit Kemp; 52-53

Mr & Mrs Robert Meyrowitz's Old Westbury house, designed by Vicente Wolf; 53 Lynn von Kersting's house in Los Angeles; 54 left designed by Terry Hunziker; 54-55 designed by Jean-Dominique Bonhotal; 55 above a riverside apartment in London, designed by Luigi Esposito; 55 below the Soho Hotel, London designed by Kit Kemp; 56 Jamie Drake's apartment in New York; 57 Eric Gizard's apartment in Paris; 58 a house in Connecticut designed by Jeffrey Bilhuber; 59 Julie Prisca's house in Normandy; 60 left and above right a cabin in Aspen, designed by Holly Lueders; 60 below a home featuring Jane Churchill fabrics; 61 a mountain retreat in Colorado, designed by Ron Mason; 62 Olivier Gagnère's apartment in Paris; 63 left designed by Collett-Zarzycki; 63 right Nathalie Lété's house in Paris, designed by Nathalie Lété; 64 a house in Italy designed by Paolo Badesco; 65 a home featuring Jane Churchill fabrics; 66 left a home featuring Jane Churchill fabrics; 66 right Mr & Mrs Sagbakken's cabin by the sea (Norway), interior design by Helene Forbes-Hennie; 67 above David Berg's house in Sweden, designed by David Berg; 67 below a home featuring Jane Churchill fabrics; 68 a home featuring Jane Churchill fabrics; 69 left a home featuring Jane Churchill fabrics; 69 right Jamie Drake's East Hampton Home; 70-71 designed by Sally Sirkin Lewis; 72 left a house in Johannesburg, designed by Johann Slee; 72 right Dominique Kieffer's house in Normandy; 73 a riverside apartment in London, designed by Luigi Esposito; 74-75 Peter Wheeler & Pascale Revert's London home, designed by Eric Gizard; 76-77 William

Cumming's house on Long Island, designed by William Cummings at Heiberg Cummings Design; 79 above left a house in Delhi, designed by Abraham & Thakore; 79 above right a house in Provence designed by Jean-Louis Raynaud & Kenyon Kramer; 79 centre a home featuring Jane Churchill fabrics; 79 below left Lena Proudlock's house in Gloucestershire; 79 below right Sera Hersham Loftus' house in London; 80 left Kenneth Wyse's house in East Hampton designed by Larry Laslo for LL Designs; 80 above right Laurence Kriegel's apartment in New York; 80 below right Designed by Pierre d'Avoine Architects; 81 James Mohn & Keith Recker's apartment in New York; architecture by James Mohn and interior design as a collaboration between Keith Recker & James Mohn; 82 Maureen Paley's house in London; 83 above left Mona Perlhagen of Chelsea Textiles' London showroom; 83 above right a house in Watermill, designed by Vicente Wolf and his associate, David Rogal; 83 below left Mrs Fasting's cabin in the Norwegian mountains, interior design by Heiberg Cummings Design; 83 below right Mr & Mrs Sagbakken's cabin by the sea (Norway), interior design by Helene Forbes-Hennie; 84 a loft apartment designed by Ushida Findlay; 86 a cabin in Aspen, designed by Holly Lueders; 87 left Frank Faulkner's house in upstate New York; 87 right a house in Delhi, designed by Abraham & Thakore; 88-89 designed by Ted Russell; 90 above an apartment in New York designed by John Barman Inc.; 90 below Baldassare La Rizza's apartment in London; 91 Gérard Faivre's apartment in Paris; 92 above left a house in Oxfordshire designed by Todhunter Earle; 92 above right William Cumming's house on Long Island, designed by William Cummings at Heiberg Cummings Design; 92 below Muriel Brandolini's home in the Hamptons, New York; 93 above a New York townhouse designed by Larry Laslo for LL Designs; 93 below the Soho Hotel, London designed by Kit Kemp; 94 Wingate Jackson, Jr and Paul Trantanella's house in upstate New York; 95 a New York townhouse designed by Larry Laslo for LL Designs; 96 Graham Head (of ABC Carpet & Home) and Barbara Rathborne's house in Long Island; 97 Mr & Mrs Stokke's cabin in the Norwegian mountains, interior design by Helene Forbes-Hennie; 98 above left a house in Delhi, designed by Abraham & Thakore; 98 above right a home featuring Jane Churchill fabrics; 98 below left Sera Hersham Loftus' house in London; 98 below right a home featuring Jane Churchill fabrics; 99 left a home featuring Jane Churchill fabrics; 99 right designer, Nathalie Hambro's apartment in London; 100 left William Cumming's house on Long Island, designed by William Cummings at Heiberg Cummings Design; 100 right Anna Bonde of Linum's house in Provence; 101 Dominique Kieffer's house in Normandy; 102-103 designed by Terry Hunziker; 105 above left Rose House, near Sydney, designed by Ian Moore Architects; 105 above right a home featuring Jane Churchill fabrics; 105 centre a home featuring Jane Churchill fabrics; 105 below left designed by Thad Hayes; 105 below right Reed & Delphine Krakoff's Manhattan townhouse, designed by Delphine Krakoff of Pamplemousse Design Inc.; 106 left Mark Rios's home in Los Angeles; 106 right Olivier Gagnère's apartment in Paris; 107 a house in Delhi, designed by Abraham & Thakore; 108 left a house in Provence designed by Jean-Louis Raynaud & Kenyon Kramer; 108 right Olivier Gagnère's apartment in Paris; 109 a house in Delhi, designed by Abraham & Thakore; 110 above a house in Suffolk, designed by James Gorst; 110 below a mountain retreat in Colorado, designed by Ron Mason; 111 James Gager & Richard Ferretti's Pennsylvanian house; 112 a home featuring Jane Churchill fabrics; 112-113 Rose House, near Syndey, designed by Ian Moore Architects; 114 Ben Langlands & Nikki Bell's house in London; 116 James Gager & Richard Ferretti's Pennsylvanian house; 117 above interior design by Kelly Hoppen; 117 below Keith & Cathy Abell's New York house designed by 1100 Architect; 118 Nina Gustafsson's Swedish home; 119 above left a home featuring Jane Churchill fabrics; 119 above right a house in Delhi, designed by Abraham & Thakore; 119 below left a home featuring Jane Churchill fabrics; 119 below right Bernie de le Cuona's Windsor house; 120 John and Marilyn Roscoe's house in California, designed by Helena Arahuete Architect of Lautner Associates; 120-121 John & Susan Wardle's house in Melbourne, designed by John Wardle Architects; 122 left a home featuring Jane Churchill fabrics; 122 right Eric Malliander's apartment in New York, designed by Eric Malliander at Resistance Design; 123 above left Penthouse loft in New York designed by Bruce Bierman Design Inc.; 123 above right the home of Carolyn van Outersterp of CVO in the North East of England; 123 below Michael Coorengel & Jean-Pierre Calvagrac's apartment in Paris; 124 left a house in East Hampton, designed by Selldorf Architects; 124 right Michael Leva's house in Connecticut; 125 Noel Berk and Liz Omedes' New York apartment, designed by Drake Design Associates; 126 designed by Andrzej Zarzycki; 127 designed by Robert Bray & Mitchell Turnbough of Bray-Schaible Design Inc.; 128 a house in Connecticut designed by Michael Trapp; 129 above left Ali Sharland's house in Gloucestershire; 129 above right Christophe Gollut's house in Gran Canaria; 129 below left Sera Hersham Loftus' house in London; 129 below right a home featuring Jane Churchill fabrics; 130 Pam Skaist-Levy of Juicy Couture's house designed by Leonardo Chalupowicz; 131 above designed by Jonathan Reed; 131 below designed by Michael Woolfson; 132 left a house in Connecticut designed by Michael Trapp; 132 right Reed & Delphine Krakoff's Manhattan townhouse, designed by Delphine Krakoff of Pamplemousse Design Inc.; 133 Lena Proudlock's house in Gloucestershire; 134 Mona Perlhagen of Chelsea Textiles' London showroom; 135 a New York townhouse designed by Larry Laslo for LL Designs; 144 a home featuring Jane Churchill fabrics;

This is the first book I've done with Jacqui Small whose work I have
long admired. It has been a real pleasure, thanks to Jacqui's direction;
my editor, Hilary Mandleberg, who manages to make everything sound
more elegant; Ashley Western, an exceptional art director, and
Nadine Bazar, an equally exceptional picture researcher. Thanks, too,
as always, to my special agents, Limelight Management.